Laura LeBrun is a jack of all trades and a master of none. Laura currently works as anything that will pay her by day and a writer by night. Her number one passion is making others laugh and making them feel good about themselves.

This book is dedicated to all the idiots in the world—I'm right here with you. And to Mulugeta Aga, who is not an idiot, but a real class act.

Laura LeBrun

CUDDLING WITH CADAVERS

AUSTIN MACAULEY PUBLISHERS™
LONDON • CAMBRIDGE • NEW YORK • SHARJAH

Copyright © Laura LeBrun 2021

The right of Laura LeBrun to be identified as author of this work has been asserted by the author in accordance with section 77 and 78 of the Copyright, Designs and Patents Act 1988.

All rights reserved. No part of this publication may be reproduced, stored in a retrieval system, or transmitted in any form or by any means, electronic, mechanical, photocopying, recording, or otherwise, without the prior permission of the publishers.

Any person who commits any unauthorized act in relation to this publication may be liable to criminal prosecution and civil claims for damages.

All of the events in this memoir are true to the best of author's memory. The views expressed in this memoir are solely those of the author.

A CIP catalogue record for this title is available from the British Library.

ISBN 9781788230643 (Paperback)
ISBN 9781788230674 (ePub e-book)

www.austinmacauley.com

First Published 2021
Austin Macauley Publishers Ltd®
1 Canada Square
Canary Wharf
London
E14 5AA
+44 (0)20 7038 8212
+44 (0)20 3515 0352

Table of Contents

Thug Life	9
Asian Nation	19
The Things We Do for Love	23
Performance: Level One	28
Cuddling with Cadavers	35
I'm in Love with David Sedaris	39
Crazy Couponing	44
Extreme Makeover Wingspan Edition	49
P.E. and Me	52
Six Times Six Equals Thirty-Six I Think	58
To Stay at Home or Not? That is the Question	63
Bitches Be Trippin'	67
Third Time is the Charm I hope	75
Final Destination: Hell	82
Hoarders: Operation Laura	87
Just Say No!	92
Lazy Eye Laura	98
My Mission	102

Mouse House and Rat Maze	109
Proud Parenting	116
Puberty is Gross	122
Sharkeisha, No!	129
The Men's Room	133
Psychopath	138
Letter to My Ex-Husband's New Wife	144

Thug Life

As a child I was a bit of a rebel. Okay, I still am, but I was even more so as a kid. One might blame the rebelliousness on being the second child. After all, we are said to be rebellious and stubborn. There is even a syndrome associated with it called 'second-child syndrome'. I follow the characteristics of second child to a T and we all know how fun it is to blame random-ass syndromes as the reason we are being a dick.

As the second out of six and the oldest daughter, I had the distinction of being 'the second mother'. I took this to heart. Not so much to nurture any of my siblings, but to boss them around. I did my best to make sure they understood I was not a role model, but a force to be reckoned with.

I had a naughty streak several miles long. Some might say I needed an exorcist at times, which, in all fairness, would have been correct. At times I could feel a demon inside me. I had a hair-trigger temper, and I often used it to scare away potential threats. Even as a child, I was a volcano of bad language; often erupting and spewing foul curses over anyone in the vicinity.

I perfected something my parents referred to as the 'tornado face'. An apt description of the fury about to be unleashed, the 'tornado face' was the exact same face made famous, years later, by the Grumpy Cat. If only I had been born 20 years later, 200 times cuter and a cat, I could've been famous for my signature look, instead of being forced to go stand with my nose in the corner for having a bad attitude.

As a side note, did anyone else have this as a childhood punishment? Along with the occasional spanking, putting my nose in a corner was sprinkled in as a consequence for crimes not quite worthy of the paddle. The punishment is self-explanatory, i.e. you stand with your nose in a corner, until the parent decides you have learned a lesson, or, as it happened in my case, until they remembered you were there.

It just so happened that my dad forgot about me one time on vacation. I had received the aforementioned consequence, only to be forgotten about when my dad fell asleep. I was no fool. I knew he could be, and almost certainly was, faking slumber in order to catch me shirking my punishment. I refused to give him the satisfaction of finding me sneaking away. I remained resolutely in that damn corner; nose pressed up against the wall.

Six hours later, my dad awoke to find me slumped against the wall, asleep. Sheepishly, he woke me; and for the rest of his life, neither of us admitted any wrongdoing. What can I say? We had a fun relationship.

One of my biggest childhood character flaws was being greedy. This may have been a by-product of being a child in a large family, or, just because I was an asshole. Regardless, I wanted stuff. If there was something to be had, I wanted it. The problem for me was getting it using legally appropriate venues.

I had chores to complete each week and was paid the appropriate child-slave wages; one to two dollars a week.

Considering we probably did a shoddy job, with our mom cleaning her way behind us, it was generous of our parents to offer us anything. But as children, we muttered under our breaths about the injustice of it all and threatened mutiny.

"Why'd they even have kids?" I remember bitterly complaining, "They probably just wanted someone to do all the work around here. Cheapskates."

Obviously, the thousands of dollars they put into birth a child, put it through school and eventually bail it out of jail, never crossed my mind.

Not being able to earn enough money from my penny-pinching parents, I took to a life of crime. Like most criminals, I started small. I decided the best way to get money was to steal oranges and apples from my parents' refrigerator and set up my own fruit stand in the driveway. Not only was this easy money, but I could look fiscally-minded.

It took less effort than making lemonade, and I could sell each piece of fruit for a whopping fifty cents each! That is, I could have if anyone had actually bought any. Instead of a fat piggy bank, I got strange looks from neighbours; and eventually a scolding and a lesson on economics from my parents.

Next, I decided I needed to not only be proactive, but a bit of a conman if I wanted success. When I think of what I did now I'm totally ashamed, but at age eight, I thought I was a fucking genius!

In my mind, every good con needed a touching sob story. In order to convince people to hand out the cash, I needed to tug on the ole heartstrings. My story, although a complete and utter lie, was fool proof: Our dog was sick. So sick that she was about to die if she didn't receive the medicine she needed.

In order to save her life, I needed donations of money to go toward her meds.

You see what a good story this is? Not only is it simple (easier to remember the lies), but it involves an animal!

No one can say no to an animal! I also knew that I alone was not cute enough to illicit enough sympathy. I needed to enlist the help of my tiny blond-haired blue-eyed doe of a sister. An added benefit was that she didn't really know what she was doing. She was the perfect prop.

Next, I chose the victims. An old couple who lived down the street. They were the sweetest people on earth. They even had matching names: Herman and Hellen. Why I would purposefully try to con the nicest people in the world can only be explained one way—my mom must've had an affair with the devil, and I was the product of that union.

My sister and I knocked on Herman and Hellen's door, and I did my best to emulate the most sombre of expressions; and to perhaps bring a shimmer of tears to my eyes.

Hellen answered, her grandmotherly presence bringing just a twinge of guilt to the surface. Nevertheless, I pressed onward with my recited tale of woe. Herman came to stand beside her, a bemused expression on his face.

"Oh dear," he said. "What exactly is wrong with your poor pup?"

"I don't really know," I confessed, "but if we don't get her the medicine, she'll die."

"My, that sounds serious," Hellen said, shaking her head sadly. "And your parents want you to come ask for money?"

It was at this point that I realized I needed to play my hand carefully.

"No," I sweetly replied, "we thought we'd surprise them with the money."

"Well, how nice," Herman said with a twinkle in his eye. "I think I might be able to help."

Jackpot!

I looked up at him, trying to look both humble and grateful for his magnanimous offering.

"I've got a good friend who's a vet. I'll give your mom a call, find out the symptoms and see if he has any ideas on how to help."

My brain leapt into panic mode. Abort! Abort! I began back peddling like it was an Olympic sport and I was going for the gold.

"No, no." I quickly assured him, "That's okay. Thanks anyway!" And with that, I grabbed my sister's arm and hauled ass down the street. I hid, the rest of the day, hoping that Herman would keep the information to himself.

Herman, that rat bastard, called my parents and told them what we were up to. My sister, as young as she was, was off the hook. I, the mastermind (though a poor one), got grounded. Possibly even nose-in-the-walled.

Deciding a career in con-artistry wasn't in the cards, I switched tactics yet again. This time, I told myself, its balls to the wall. Do or die. (I had recently learned these phrases, and I relished trying them out as often as I could.)

I began stealing spare change from my mom's purse. A dime here, a nickel there. Never bills, and rarely quarters, as these are easily noticed when missing. But this wasn't enough for the greed-monster inside of me. Especially when a new toy came out—Puppy in my Pocket.

Oh, what can I say about Puppy in my Pocket? I was in love. They may have been just miniature dog figurines, but I was a girl obsessed. When the package said to 'Collect them all!' I took this as a command, not a fun suggestion. The problem was, they were $4.99 a pop, and my child-slave job didn't create Puppy in my Pocket kind of cash. Nor did my mom's purse yield the required dividends. I knew what I had to do. I was going to shoplift.

I knew shoplifting was wrong, just as I knew stealing from my mom's purse and conning old people was wrong. The thing was, I didn't care. To me (devil that I was), the ends justified the means. Those Puppy in my Pockets would be mine.

Our small little town didn't sell Puppy in my Pockets, but the city 35 minutes away did. And, it just so happened that my family went to that city at least twice a week—for church. Ignoring the religious irony, I hatched a plan.

In order to understand my plan, you need to understand a bit about Mormon church meetings. Every Sunday, Mormons meet for three hours; three meetings lasting an hour each. The first meeting, Sacrament, is everyone together. The second two are divided, adults from children. I decided that when all my fellow children were off to learn about Jesus and choosing the right, I'd be off to shoplift.

I was only brave enough to contemplate this because my strict-as-anything father was gone, headed to visit another congregation in a neighbouring town. My poor mom, saddled with multiple unruly children, was just trying to keep us corralled and not committing any crimes. Little did she know, am I right?

After Sacrament meeting let out, I hid in the bathroom until I could sneak out without anyone seeing. Once the coast was clear, I took off, running the first block or so, trying to get as far away as possible without anyone seeing me.

Four blocks away was the intended target: Shopko. I figured I'd be inconspicuous, a child in the store with her mother, browsing the toy aisle. I was wearing a dress, so I was extra innocent looking. In the toy aisle, I gathered as many boxes of Puppy in my Pockets as possible, and, turning away from any onlookers, shoved them under my dress.

After seeing the unsightly bulges they created, I knew that I wouldn't be able to get away with this. I took them out and rethought my strategy. I came up with something better. Looking lost, I'd take them into the bathroom, pretending to look for my mom. If caught, I'd tell them I didn't see the sign demanding no unpaid merchandise in the restroom. I was, after all, scared and lost.

Ignoring any questioning looks, I headed into the restroom. Seeing some feet in one of the two stalls, I entered a stall, determined to wait out the phantom pooper next to me. Once she had finished, she washed up and left. The moment I heard the door close behind her, I ripped into those packages like a kid at Christmas. Well, a kid at Christmas who was forced to open difficult packages as quietly as possible, in a public restroom.

I threw the packages into the trash, covering them with toilet paper so they wouldn't be discovered right away. Then I set about finding a place to hide the figurines. Really, I should have thought it through before stealing more than I could carry. I had no pockets, and it was summer, so no sweater or coat was needed. Luckily, I had underwear.

I began putting Puppy in my Pockets in my underwear, trying to find the spots that were least obvious to the watchful eye. Once again, my greed got the best of me, and I had more little puppies then space in my panties. They ballooned out in tiny dog-shaped tumours. Due to the large quantity of stolen goods, I'd also have to waddle, which would definitely be suspicious.

I've said it before and I'll say it again. My intelligence seems to lean to the wicked, so I knew, even at such a young age, I wasn't likely to be stopped by anyone. After all, what would they do? Demand to look inside an eight-year-old girl's underwear? I think not. The lawsuits that could result would not be worth the $30 or so stolen by the little vagabond.

Taking a deep breath, I waddled out of the bathroom slowly. Trying to not look guilty, I even stopped and took a drink from the water fountain before I exited the store. Balls to the wall was I! Just call me lil gangsta Laura.

I picked up my pace after leaving the store, trying to get as far away as possible. How far would the law follow me? Would they tail me all of the way to the church? I purposefully took wrong turns, just to double back when I was sure no one was following. At one point, I realized I had been losing my load, leaving dog-shaped droppings in my wake. I had to hurry back, following my Hansel and Gretel like trail of puppy crumbs until I had recollected all my prizes.

As I entered the parking lot to our church, I stopped to look at my illegally gained loot. As I was making sure all of my babies had survived the trip, I suddenly froze, hand in underwear. I heard the unmistakable sound of my father's voice.

I peeked around the van I was hiding behind. He was there! He had stopped to chat with a man from our church. I panicked! I could not let him see me. I was supposed to be in class! I looked for an escape. The building was too far away, and he would see me if I attempted to run to it. There was nothing to hide behind, but there was something to hide under.

I began to shimmy under the van next to me, my Sunday dress snagging on the uneven pavement. Heart beating wildly, I ignored the puppies digging into the crack of my butt. I held my breath as my dad pulled into the parking spot right next to the van. (*Of course he'd do that*, I thought. *Out of all the empty parking spots in the entire damn lot!*)

I watched, in utter terror, as his feet got out of the car, then slowed to a stop. Had he seen me? Were my feet sticking out like the Wicked Witch of the East, after the house dropped on her? I struggled to repress a sigh as he continued, on his way.

After waiting just long enough for him to enter, I shimmied back out, paranoid he had developed the ability to levitate, and would be hovering over me. He was not, enabling me to waddle-run and hide behind the nearest tree.

I stood, afraid for my life, until I heard an "ahem..." behind me. I jumped, dropping a few of my puppies from their pocket (my underwear) as I did so.

An older gentleman stared at me and asked what I was doing. I told him I was playing a game, and he told me I was standing in his flowerbed.

I looked down, ashamed to see I was, in fact, squashing several beautiful flowers. I hopped off them, shamefaced and decided I'd have to take my chances inside the church. I apologized as I hobbled off and ducked into the church.

Luckily, there was a bathroom right by the entrance. I hid there for the remaining block of church, too terrified to move, lest I cause myself even more trouble. I decided then and there that a life of crime was not for me. It was too much work.

My mother, not being the oblivious moron I'd assumed (hoped?) she was, figured out quickly that I had stolen my precious puppies. She made me apologize and pay back the store. Honestly, I was relieved. I couldn't take the pressure of being a hardened criminal. It was disappointing though, that I was not the evil genius I thought I was. After all, evil geniuses get away with their deeds, not caught with mini-poodles in their pantaloons.

Asian Nation

Today I unexpectedly found myself in a situation I could never have imagined. Due to some miscommunication between myself and the Vietnamese speaking masseuse I had hired, I ended up face down on a table while she pulled my dress top down and unhooked my bra.

Let me back up a bit. There is a place in my town called Foot Spa, where for a mere $35, you can get an hour-long foot massage performed by Asian women who really know their shit. You don't have to make an appointment, and there is never a wait. You lay down, soak your feet while your shoulders and head are massaged, all the while listening to birds chirping and harps playing. Once your feet are officially defunkified, the masseuse gets to work on fixing all your life's ailments. My life seems to be riddled with problems, so I find myself there once every few months.

The Foot Spa has several different options, one of which is the 45-minute foot massage and 15-minute back massage, though usually I pick the 60-minute foot reflexology, because as adorable as my feet are, it seems the only people I can get to touch them are people I pay.

So there I was, blissed out of my mind with people touching my tootsies, when I think she tells me my massage is over. I grab my stuff and stand to leave, when I make out, "No, facedown." Never being one to refuse the requests of a sweet Asian, I did as she commanded and laid facedown. Suddenly, the top of my maxi-dress was being pulled down to my butt and she was unhooking my bra like a fucking expert!

It was then I realized that even if she had a nefarious purpose in mind, I wasn't about to say no. I knew, due to previous exposure to Asian women's hands, that I was going to like whatever she had in mind. As her freakishly strong hands worked on the many knots in my shoulders, I decided I was in heaven.

Now, I'm not saying I'm gay, but I'm also not saying I'm not gay. Because when she put her hands on me, I seriously considered dumping my fiancé and asking her to marry me. I could give her a happy life. I was sure of it. And strangely enough, it wasn't the first time I felt the impulse to propose to an Asian woman.

When I was a good little Mormon missionary serving in Sydney, Australia, my mission companion and I often got our haircut in 'Korea-town'. If I had more hair, I would have gone to get it cut every day, thanks to the sexy-ass scalp massage the women would give while washing the hair. During the massage I would receive goosebumps that would last for days. I remember laying there thinking about how I would give my left breast for this woman to follow me wherever I went, massaging my scalp. I would forever be unsatisfied with future haircuts from the moment she ran her fingers through my hair.

Unfortunately, we, women who are not of Asian descent, are screwed. Because these women have got it down! It is impossible to compete with them, especially when it comes to men.

When I started dating my fiancé, he mentioned that his type was short, thin, with small breasts. Because I knew he was a fan of anime, I knew he meant 'Asian'. I almost gave up on him at that moment, because if there was an opposite of what I look like, it would be Mulan.

I am neither short (I'm 5' 10") or thin, (my body fat index moves up and down with regularity) and my boobs are, um, hefty. Not porn star big-and-bouncy; just middle-aged-nursed-to-death melons. My skin is not smooth, and my eyes are not almond. I am not graceful or musically gifted, and I know nothing about anime.

Before you get on your high horse, yes, I realize many of these are generalizations, but they are positive ones, so don't get your panties in a twist. I'm complimenting, okay? Geez.

The point is, ladies, we cannot compete against Asian women for the affections of men. They are superior in every way. Disagree? Prove me wrong. But never fear! I have a plan! Instead of competing against the women, we will compete for the women. Against the men. Yes, we will all have to become lesbians, but trust me, once you've felt those tiny hands on your feet or scalp, you won't regret it.

I think we have a chance, ladies! I mean, think about it! Who knows how to treat a woman better than another woman? We will most assuredly be nicer to them than the big bad men in their lives, and we would fully appreciate everything they can do. And I bet we will be better at helping around the house than your typical dude is.

We won't be sad if we get pregnant and have a daughter, because that just means the world is gaining one more fantastic masseuse. If we borrow sperm from our gay brothers, perhaps we could eventually rid the world of straight men completely. Just something to think about. Wink, wink.

Sadly, despite what religion may claim, we can't just up and choose to be gay. So, we will have to work with what we've got and hope that there is an odd bird out there who will happily choose our trash-eating-pigeon to their gracefully-gliding-crane.

The Things We Do for Love

One day at work, I found myself chasing a huge cockroach around the women's restroom with my lunchbox. It might have been the largest I've ever seen, with eyes the size of marbles and the body the size of a small rabbit. My intentions were to capture it in my lunchbox and bring it home for my fiancé.

"Get in there you little shit," I angrily commanded as I chased it behind the toilet. I grumbled to myself and banged around noisily, trying to not touch anything while trapping the bug.

I heard a timid, "You okay in there?" coming from the next stall. I mentally slapped myself. I must have missed the other woman entering while I was focused on my mission. Realizing it must sound like I was talking to my poop, my face flamed bright red and I gave an embarrassed chuckle.

"Oh, yeah. Um, I'm trying to catch this big roach and bring it home for my fiancé." As soon as I said this, I realized how certifiably insane I sounded. I fumbled for words, attempting to make it better with, "he has a bunch of ants he keeps, and this one could provide a lot of meat for them." I was met with silence. Silence I met with more unappreciated verbal diarrhoea.

"I personally hate bugs, so I'm trying to be brave and catch this. You know, it's like when a man comes home with a big fish he caught for dinner. The woman is all proud, right? Or at least she pretends to be, male egos being what they are and all. Anyhow, I plan to bring it home so my fiancé realizes I'm cool. This cockroach could be the one thing preventing him from leaving me for a younger and thinner woman who likes bugs. Good plan, right?"

Nothing.

I cleared my throat. "I'm sure I sound crazy, but it is just one of those things you do for love, ya know? I mean, who hasn't chased a Godzilla roach around a public bathroom for a man, right?" Once again, there was no response. I looked under the stall and saw nothing. Either she had put her feet up on the toilet seat and was hiding until the bug chasing psycho in the next stall left, or she had scurried away from me faster than the roach I seemed to have lost track of. I couldn't blame her.

Attempting to corral gargantuan insects was neither the first, nor the last strange thing I have done for love. Like many women, I try to please the men in my life with every trick in the book. If he loves sports, I will watch football along with him, wearing appropriate sports-like apparel, and pretending to know the difference between a court and a field. Is there one? I will smile and nod when he shouts, "Did you see that?" when I have absolutely no idea what he is talking about because I was picking at my toenails and dreaming of what to eat for second lunch. I will try to stay awake during football games, when I am dying a little inside every time the game stops, which is apparently every two seconds. Why is football so damn slow? It seems to consist of spitting, side-line standing and pompous sports announcers shouting their opinions over each other. No, thank you. Not for me. I can enjoy soccer, with its constant movement, sexy legs, and academy award winning flops. But unfortunately for me, Texas in known for being obsessed with football.

In elementary school, I had so many crushes I couldn't possibly remember them all. I do remember trying to please all of them with various changes to my wardrobe, looks, and personality. When those changes inevitably didn't work, I plied them with ~~bribes~~ gifts, hoping to win their love. In the fifth grade, there was a boy named Tyler Penning that I just adored. He was popular and very cute, with the political clout to move me from being bullied to being the bully.

Being the smart-but-clueless-girl I was, I used his cousin Jill to find out more about him. Discovering he liked ghost stories, I realized our love was meant to be! I liked ghost stories, too! In fact, I had recently acquired a collection of scary stories; the pinnacle of my prized possessions.

The moment I found out he liked spooky stories, I ran home and wrapped my collection in the Sunday comics. I smiled, just knowing he would find my wrapping job clever and frugal. Inside the wrapped-up package I included a note that said, "I like you. Do you like me? Check yes or no." Yeah, yeah, I know. How very bourgeois and cliché. But it's what I did. So sue me. The following day at school, I slipped the present into Tyler's desk and eagerly awaited his reaction.

When I finally got the reaction I was anticipating, I was underwhelmed. He saw the package, shrugged, and put it into his backpack, as if it were just another average day. Oh, the life of attractive people! You better believe I'd do more than shrug at such a thoughtful gift. I nearly kneeled at my boyfriend's feet when he brought me a Diet Coke.

The next day, I was delighted to discover a note in my desk, folded up in the manner of all childhood notes; a triangle. When I was sure no one was watching, I unfolded the paper and found the note I had included in his gift. On it, the box 'No' was checked multiple times in red marker. He made sure there was no confusion or hope. The check marked box was a kick to my silly ten-year-old heart. And while he certainly returned my note, he didn't, however, return the books. I was bitter about that for years, never knowing if I could demand them back. News flash: you can't demand someone return a gift. According to Emily Post, it simply isn't done.

In high school, I had a mad crush on a gorgeous guy from California who had a thing for short-haired brunettes. At the time, I had beautiful, long honey-coloured hair. But for this dangerous new stranger's love, and without a second thought, I chopped off all my hair and dyed it a hideous shade of brown. Well, it was supposed to be brown, but ended up looking more 'goblin green' than 'chestnut brown'.

Apparently, he had a thing for short-haired brunettes that were, unfortunately, not me. No matter what I did with my hair, he would never have a 'thing' for me. I did donate my hair to a charity, so hopefully something good came from my teenage heartbreak and subsequent awful hairstyles.

I'm not proud of it, but I've pretended to like terrifying things like spiders and exercise to get the attention of a guy I liked. Thankfully my desire to impress them usually seemed to be too much effort after only a short time. Laziness to the rescue again.

With my fiancé, it's different. While I don't like catching bugs, I'll do it happily for him. I'll wash and fold his laundry (even though he never asks me to), do his dishes, grocery shopping and other obnoxious daily tasks. As it just so happens, love makes me into a kinder, more generous person. I even gave up 70% of my wardrobe so he could have room for his clothes in my closet. You'd think I should be up for sainthood, but I really just wear the same two pairs of sweatpants every day, so it wasn't a huge sacrifice.

Of course, it goes both ways, swinging wildly in my favor. My fiancé puts up with my mood swings and my intensely passionate opinions about things that don't matter in the slightest. He will smile and pat me on the shoulder when I loudly proclaim my distaste over people who earn money playing games on the internet. What kind of job is that? (Yes, I'm just jealous.) He doesn't run away screaming when I yammer on and on about how the world is full of idiots, then promptly stub my toe on a piece of furniture that has been there for years.

In truth, he has it much harder than I do. He deals with my crazy, and in return I help him catch bugs. I've got the better end of the deal for sure. At least I can use gloves and a box to deal with my end. He's not as lucky. And it just so happens that I like the version of myself he brings to the surface. It feels more authentic, more free. I can be myself; not changing my personality but adding to it. I suppose this is love. I'm digging it. It is totally worth a roach-chase or two.

Performance: Level One

I feel bad for old people. I really do. I often remind myself that I don't want to live to be old, though what 'old' is, I'm not quite sure. Maybe I'll be old when I'm in my nineties, or maybe I'll be old in a couple years. Who can tell? I figure I'll know when the time comes. And when the time comes, I've got a bottle of sleeping pills and a trip up Mt McKinley to hypothermia town all planned out.

I love old people, I really do. But I don't love smelling them. I feel bad saying it, but there really is an older person smell. Perfume de sadness. If you combine old people and taking piano lessons from them, you get my experiences with Ms Koch.

Ms Koch was (I'm using past tense, as I assume she has since met the grim reaper) a short squat little woman in her 70s. Or 80s. Hell if I know. To me, she seemed ancient. She had the typical hairdo popular with those of her age, the spiral perm fluffed out to poodle proportions and dyed an unnatural shade of apricot. She had taught music in school, then moved on to teach private piano lessons in our town when my family discovered her; much to my father's delight and me and my siblings' chagrin.

My father was excited because he desired for his children the same opportunity for misery he himself faced as a child. He and his seven siblings were forced to practice the piano for (according to him) an hour a day, though the math doesn't seem to quite add up with this, and I don't know how his mom could have stood listening to that all day.

Not only did his family play the piano, they were also proficient in playing the marimba; performing different functions around the state, not unlike the Partridge family. Only less well known and much more 'Mormon'. They were a musically talented family, and according to dad, put forth the kind of dedication and effort it takes to become so. I was not nearly as focused.

Though I dreamed (like most little girls) of becoming a famous singer/songwriter; the kind with swarms of fans and millions of dollars, I didn't actually want to put forth the work to become any better at it. And, when I did try to learn and improve, I found I had very little natural talent. While with enough laborious plunking away I could become proficient in the right hand, then the left, I could not, for the life of me, tie them together in a way that my brain would allow. For me, my right hand was English, and my left-hand Math—the two always at odds with one another.

Every week Ms Koch assigned us music pieces to work on, expecting improvement the following lesson. She would often assign me music that was less advanced than my younger siblings, which really got me all sorts of offended. Truthfully, she was in the right, seeing as how I had little talent to boast, but it still hurt my pride. I would be fumbling through songs that my younger brother had passed months ago, though he was two years my junior. Watching everyone surpass me gave me very little motivation to do better or try harder.

Every week, my mom would lure me to my piano lesson with promises of chocolate milk and a donut. Though I pretended to consider it heavily, I was a cheap buy, caving in every time, dreaming of chocolate and carbs.

I'd slowly lumber into Ms Koch's house, and immediately my nostrils would be assaulted with the smell of sulphur; the special kind Satan keeps in his torture chambers. For the life of me, I could not figure out what Ms Koch could have eaten to give her such noxious gas. And she had to have known her home was permeated with it, right? I mean, how on earth could you not know your home smells like the Devil's lair? Did she just get used to it and forget it existed? Had her olfactory senses failed her due to advanced age? Or, and this is the scenario I find most likely, did she do it on purpose, as some sort of passive aggressive 'fuck you' to her students, to me in particular?

Ms Koch did not like me. I want to say I had no idea why, but I'm sure I do. I was not motivated, I lied about practicing every single week, and I often gave up in the middle of the song, not wanting to butcher it anymore in front of an audience, even if the audience was just an old crone. She would admonish me each time, telling me I would never get better with a give up attitude.

Little did she know, that give up attitude had been beaten into me after several humiliating experiences with 'confidence'. In fact, I used to have such a can-do attitude, I would do things that I did not know how to do. And I would do it with panache.

Half way through first grade, my family moved to a small town in Northwest Iowa. For some unsubstantiated reason, I was pretty sure I was hot shit; me with my pirate eye patch and Alaska sized confidence. Especially when it came to the arts. I saw myself as one step away from stardom, constantly searching for my 'big break'.

In music class, we would have a talent show case twice a year. The moment it was time to get volunteer performers, my hand would shoot up in the air faster than Hitler's. The first time, I announced I knew how to play 'Mary Had a Little Lamb' on the piano, when, in fact, I did not. Ms Hector, our underpaid and overstressed teacher, waved me up to the piano.

With a flourish, I sat down, stretching out my fingers and appropriating the right posture. Then I began to play something that, while at first it seemed like it could possibly be 'Mary Had a Little Lamb', turned into an unrecognizable blob of sound by note four. I was really getting going when Ms Hector waved me off and huffed, "That's enough. Let's let someone, who really knows how to play, have a turn." My face burned with shame as I slunk to my seat, vowing revenge. I'd show her.

The next year, I planned to perform a 'freestyle' (made up as I went) dance to 'The Phantom of the Opera'. It was a lot of arm waving and hand gestures, with some dramatic leaps and twirls thrown in to show off my ballerina-like skill. While at the time I imagined myself looking like an artsy off-Broadway dancer, in truth I looked like a drunken Hippopotamus, my leaps less delicate and more dinosaurian.

Once my dance was performed, the last notes of the music fading away to the embarrassed and awkward silence of my fellow first graders, Ms Hector cleared her throat and attempted a compliment.

"Thank you, Laura. That was very, uh, creative."

As I took a final bow, I lorded over my fellow elementary students, knowing that their feeble attempts to outperform me would be futile.

"No bow necessary, Laura. Take your seat."

Apparently, her charitable spirit was short lived.

Ms Koch had a similar mindset. She, obnoxiously, required her students to actually know what they performed at her semi-annual 'recitals' (two-hour long torture fests). In order to not be embarrassed by me, she would assign me songs a catatonic monkey could play.

I'd be sitting, in my fine Sunday dress, listening to all the younger kids perform their pieces (the order went youngest to oldest) and I would realize I would be playing a much easier song than theirs, even though I was several years older. My hands would start to shake, and I would feel vomit creeping up my throat. Eventually, it would be my turn and I would butcher my song as fast as possible, sick with shame at the forced applause.

The day I quit piano for good was a doozy. I threw caution to the wind, knowing I was risking parental fury, but testing the waters anyway. Let me set the scene. It was the recital we performed in the old folk's home, which we did once a year. We would be sitting waiting to play and would hear an elderly person yell out, "Is it over yet?" or, "This is terrible!" All while smelling human decay and bitterness mixed with bleach and dementia.

Listening to the criticism from the audience did nothing to settle my nerves. There would be no polite clapping here, but critical comments and bodily function noises. What I had once assumed would be kind grandparental support turned out to be academy award winning heckling.

I was fifteen, and extremely self-conscious, hating everything about myself. Ms Koch had assigned me, once again, a song straight from 'Piano Playing for Dummies'. I was not excited, but willing to play, if only for the fear of what would happen if I didn't. (I have subsequently found that much of my life is lived this way.)

As I waited for my turn, a seven-year-old boy took the stage. Shortly after he started, I realized he was playing the exact same song I was supposed to play! Not only was this kid half my age, he played the song a million times better than I ever could! I was going to look like a fool, and worse, the old people were going to be mean to me.

So, I did what any mature fifteen-year old would do. I ran out of the recital hall. As I was about to exit the building, Ms Koch grabbed me by the collar. With Frankenstein strength, she started dragging me back into the hall.

"No!" I yelled like a petulant toddler, "You can't make me! I won't do it!" Right at the moment I was contemplating the consequences of knocking an old lady on her ass, my mom stepped in. With her soothing voice and calm demeanour, my mom saved the day, convincing Ms Koch that I was sorry (I wasn't) and that I would be better at our next lesson (wrong again).

The money spent for lessons with Ms Koch wasn't a complete waste, as I did learn from her. I learned that sometimes it is best to quit while you are ahead, or behind in my case. I learned that it takes hard work, dedication, and a bit of natural talent, to be good at whatever it is in life that you want to excel in. And, most importantly, I learned to always be aware of what my gastrointestinal tract is producing.

Cuddling with Cadavers

"Hey...hey!" I gently shook my fiancé.

"What? I'm trying to sleep," he grumbled.

"I have a question."

"Laura, it is the middle of the night."

"I know, but it is important."

"What?"

"Okay," I began, ready to ease my mind. "If a giant came and picked me up by the head, how much would my body have to weigh for my head to pop off with my spine still attached?"

"What? This is the important question you just had to have answered in the middle of the night? Are you serious?"

"Well it is keeping me up. I need to know."

With an irritated grumble, he turned around and pulled the sheets up over his head. I was left, answerless, with no foreseeable sleep in my future. I would have to do some calculations.

Obviously, the force of the giant's grab would come into play. Maybe how hard he squeezed the head in order to pick me up, and how hard I fought back. As I laid there, I realized it would be nearly impossible for a pea-brain such as I to calculate all of this. Unless I wanted to do some serious math,

I would have to go without the answer. I had been banking on my smarty-pants partner to just give me the answer. It was really quite rude of him to just leave me hanging.

In his defence, if I must, I do wake him up often with many other important questions of a similar ilk. I've asked him why he never told me my face was the exact shape of Mr Potato Head's body, (a realization I had after getting my new driver's license photo) and, if koalas have smooth brains and are remarkably stupid, why were my lumpy thighs not celebrated for being incredibly smart? Why do people want to have stupid thighs? Huh? Tell me that, why don't ya?

Is it my fault that I have an inquiring mind? I don't think so. I believe he should be thanking his lucky stars that he gets to cuddle up next to someone so full of life and spunk. Unlike me. I have to cuddle with a cadaver.

Okay, not really. But let me tell you something about my fiancé. He is cold! His body temperature seems to hover in around twenty degrees Fahrenheit. (On a side note, have you ever spelled Fahrenheit? It took me several tries and a Google look up to get that word right.)

I will often be minding my own business, nearly asleep like the perfect little angel I am, when a horrible deathlike hand comes and curves around my belly. Immediately, my innards turn to ice and I begin the process of hypothermia.

He doesn't seem to care that I am dying from the inside out. In fact, he finds my startled yelps and fetal position curling amusing. He enjoys holding me closer as I wriggle, desperate to get away from his reptilian body. That's right, honey, I just compared you to a reptile. Yes, I know you'll take that as a compliment. Weirdo.

As you can see, I have my fair share of problems at night, lest you feel too sorry for him. Yes, I also ask important questions, and when he does answer, he usually riles me up into a fierce debate over whatever topic I had innocently brought up.

Just last night we got into a raging debate over whether or not vampires were dead or undead. I rabidly argued the undead side, while he determined that you had to be dead in order to be undead. This conversation actually came about after I told him lying in bed with him was like lying next to a corpse.

This most obnoxious part of this is that he doesn't even really care about the debate. He just likes to see me, sleepy-eyed and half asleep, emerge from my Zen-like state and morph into a raging lunatic over why he doubted I could make a human suit out of people's skin like Buffalo Bill in The Silence of the Lambs. He really can be a wiener.

I've never been a good sleeper. It takes hours for my mind to calm itself down enough for me to drift off to sleep. Usually, I'll spend the time before sleeping running things over and over in my head; my anxiety bouncing around like a kid on crack.

I may replay the day's events, mentally thrashing myself for the many stupid things I say and do. Other times I will imagine myself as an outlaw, hiding from the fuzz, living my life on the lam. Usually though, my brain hops from topic to topic, never really finishing a thought. One minute I'll be thinking about Brussel sprouts, and the next pondering if it is possible to kill someone with a thumb tack.

As young girls, my sister and I would make up stories each night before bed. Ninety-five percent of them involved cute guys we knew and our subsequent happily-ever-afters. Occasionally, I would terrify her with some of my twisted tales, and we would spend the next several minutes hiding under the covers before one of us got brave enough to turn on the lights. (To be honest, I usually made her do it, even though she is almost six years my junior. I was always disturbingly okay with sacrificing my siblings to various murderers and monsters that may have been lurking in the room.)

The moral of the story is that my fiancé has a circulation problem and should probably get that checked out. Also, that cuddling with him is like cuddling with a cadaver. (Insert sympathy for me here.) Oh, and that I can't properly finish a thought. Just like the time…Wait, what are we talking about? I'm pretty sure I remember Brussel sprouts. Oh well. I'm tired. I'm gonna go curl up next to my very own icebox. Mmmmm…cake.

I'm in Love with David Sedaris

"Hello there." I heard the voice behind me and nearly dropped dead. I'd recognize that voice anywhere! Holy shit! What was David Sedaris doing at the McDonald's inside Walmart in my small Texas town? I turned, trying to look casual, not quite able to pull it off.

"Hi! How are you?" The excitement uncontained, I gushed my greeting to none other than his Royal Highness, David Sedaris.

Only, it wasn't him.

The man who had greeted me while filling his Coke, looked a bit surprised at my overexuberant greeting, but continued on.

"It sure is hot outside. I don't care if they say it's only 95 degrees. It feels like 125 to me." The man, average looking, about six inches shorter than me, and well, around the age 80, was very sweet. He had kind eyes and a friendly demeanour, but he wasn't my idol. His voice though! I could have sworn that it had the smooth undertones of Mr Sedaris himself. While not devastated, (I am always up for an overly friendly conversation with a stranger at the Coke machine) I was disappointed David and I weren't about to bond over a nice cold beverage on a hot Texas day. The voice-doppelganger and I had a bit of a conversation, then headed in different directions, off to go about whatever it is two people do when they realize they didn't get to meet their celebrity crush and unknowing best friend.

In the car, I got to thinking. Boy, do I love David Sedaris! I really and truly do. How cool would that have been if it had actually been him! I'd follow him everywhere! (My fiancé says I should tell those unclassed fools out there who David is, but I refuse. Go look him up. You won't be sorry).

He needn't worry though. I'm too lazy to be a stalker, and too poor to do anything about it even if I weren't. Nor would I want to scare him off. Instead, I would lure him into my web of friendship, then wrap him up and make him my ~~victim~~ friend. We would run off together and live happily ever after. I'd laugh uproariously at his every witty observation and encourage him to not worry so much about what other people are thinking. Then he'd call me a hypocrite, because I'm the worst at not caring what other people think. And we would laugh and laugh. Meanwhile, Hugh would smile bemusedly at this new dynamic in his relationship. But he'd be cool with it, because obviously we would become good friends. After all, we'd have to, seeing as how we would be in a strange sandwich-like relationship. I am the peanut butter and the jelly, separating the two pieces of bread, but enhancing their flavour. Ahhh…the dream!

It has been this way for ages; me being attracted to men that are gay. How can you blame me? Gay men are notoriously good-looking, smart, and are sassy enough to make you laugh and feel good about yourself at the same time. They remind you of all wonderful qualities you have, just like your girlfriends do; only you don't have to secretly compete with them.

My first gay crush (is there a word for that?) was a kid in elementary school named Caleb. He had ginger hair and the nicest button up shirts in the entire school. He was even known to sport a sassy suspender getup now and then. If I had been a more world-wise girl, I would have seen the signs. But, being the little Mormon girl that I was, I didn't know what 'gay' was.

I yearned after Caleb because he was just so darn nice. He was kind of shy, had a fantastic sense of style (the suspenders really cinched the deal for me), and a nice smile. I tried to trick him into being my boyfriend, but, like most gay men, he was too smart for that. When he told me he didn't like girls, I just assumed he meant it in the way that all second-grade boys don't like girls. Cooties and whatnot.

I eventually got over Caleb and moved on to other gay crushes, mostly found (stereotypically) in my theatre and choir classes. We sang and acted our way around confusing feelings, never quite touching on the subject of sexuality. Needless to say, I never got around to dating any of these guys.

It wasn't until college that I got the nerve to ask anyone out. I was in a Master's Program Psychology class, even though I was just a sophomore. I'm not sure how I was able to sneak in there, but I thought it would be easy. I was wrong. Not only did I only understand two out of every five words spoken, I was the least interesting person in the class. Everyone there seemed to have a fascinating and diverse life story.

I was most intrigued with a guy named Garrison. I found his name alone to be worth exploring. He was very mysterious; only speaking to say something that blew everyone's mind. I watched him out of the corner of my eye for a few weeks before I got the courage (if you could call it that) to ask him out. Being the mature and savvy woman I was, I wrote him a note. It said something like, "I think you are so amazingly smart. And cute too! Would you like to go out with me sometime?"

Like a ninja, I slipped it to him after class one day. Then I got the hell out of dodge, because I did not want to be there when he read it. The next time we had a class, he handed me his own note. I knew then that I adored him. Because whatever his response was, at least he had stooped to my level of passing notes in class.

"Laura," it read, "I think you are such a wonderful young lady. You are smart and funny and beautiful. But you aren't for me. It isn't that I don't like you, or that I wouldn't date you under different circumstances, but I'm gay, and I'm currently in a happy relationship. Thank you for the flattering note, and I hope we can be friends. Sincerely, Garrison."

Oh, how I loved him even more after that note! He spared my feelings by letting me read my rejection in private, cushioning it with so many compliments it couldn't devastate me. This, I tell you, is true class. It is the epitome of how a man should turn down a woman. It was ions better than the time I asked a guy if he wanted to hang out and he said, I quote, "Ewww, gross. No."

After Garrison, I was better at sniffing out the gay guys. I did this by asking myself, "Am I attracted to them?" If I was, and they were nice, they were gay. Later in my college years

I did go on a few dates with a guy who was extremely gay, but afraid to admit it. I was happy to play the part of his beard for a time, but eventually he came out. As proud of him as I was, I was a bit disappointed, knowing I'd be losing him to a man.

It remains to be seen if I will ever stop lusting after gay men. But my adoration of David Sedaris comes naturally. He is a gifted wordsmith; smart and funny in his observations of people and life. His attention to detail rivals even the best of writers, always leaving me wanting more. I listen to his books on CD while driving to and from work, making the drive more bearable. I curl up with his books at night when I need something to smile about, and to dream of. So, I guess what I'm saying is, I'm in love with David Sedaris. We could have a good thing. If only he weren't just so darn gay.

Crazy Couponing

Have you ever gotten your keys stuck in a newspaper machine? I have. It took me three days and fifteen phone calls to get them back. I've also searched through recycle bins, public trash cans, and asked everyone I knew for their leftover Sunday papers. Why, you ask? Well, at one point in my life, I was a crazy couponing lady.

That's right folks. I was the obnoxious lady in the store with about fourteen coupons for each transaction, and I had three transactions. People would get in line behind me and roll their eyes. One lady even offered to give me the money I'd save with coupons to get the hell out of the way. I didn't take her up on it, because I'm nothing if not a stickler for 'the principal of the matter'.

It all began with a move to Southern California—the land of unaffordable living. I knew no one and had no money. It turns out being a full-time mom is a poorly paying profession. Eventually, I unashamedly begged another mom to be my friend while at a Burger King play place. Luckily for me, she agreed. Hi, Marlana!

Marlana confessed to me she was just getting into couponing. She had purchased a binder with card holders inside, and coupons filling each slot. I was impressed. I wanted in. And because I have never learned how to do things in moderation, I dove head first into the couponing madness.

Spending more than I was saving, I subscribed to both Sunday papers, purchased a binder and card holders, and spent hours clipping coupons and putting them into their allotted slots. Marlana and I often bonded over the snipping and folding sounds that came from all our hard work. We would talk about kids, husbands, and how they all drove us crazy. When I think about it now, I'm pretty sure we were using couponing as a form of therapy.

Together we scoured websites to find the best deals, then obsessively waited outside each store for them to open so we could get the best deals before other 'couponers' could swoop in and snatch them up first. We aggressively made our way to the items and argued with cashiers when they didn't know their own coupon policies as well as we did.

After all of that, we'd walk away feeling victorious, knowing we got away with legal highway robbery. It was such a high that Marlana and I started our own couponing website, helping others get the best deals in the area, and perhaps the country. We were riding high on the waves of saving money.

The problem was, in order to 'save' money, I had to spend it. Meaning that I ended up buying a lot of stuff I didn't need, just because I could get them cheaply. I had closets full of deodorant and toothpaste, but not enough armpits to de-stank or teeth to de-plaque. I had more items than room to store them. The kind and generous soul I am, I decided to donate what I had to people in need.

Weirdly enough, it was hard to find places that would accept my donations. I suppose we live in a day and age where everyone's motives are suspect. Why did I want to donate 60 tubes of toothpaste? Because I have them, and someone could benefit from them. Apparently, I look like the type of person who wants to poison people via deodorant. You know me, just out to terrorize the world, one armpit at a time.

After amounts of questioning usually reserved for people at Guantanamo Bay, my donations would be accepted and delivered to people in need, and I would feel good about myself until my husband asked me why I was spending so much on body wash and shampoo.

"Because you can get it for only 45 cents a bottle!"

"But we don't need it. And 45 cents add up when you are buying 40 bottles."

We stood at an impasse, not knowing what to do with the other, but understanding we were the only sane one in the relationship. Truth be told, I knew that the money was adding up, and space in our home was being subtracted, but I couldn't stop. I was addicted.

I bought food we wouldn't eat, and household items we'd never use. I bought, and I bought, and I bought. I wasted hours upon hours driving from store to store and looking up sale items. I was in the throes of an addiction, and I didn't know how to stop.

Eventually, we moved to Utah, land of the cheapest people known to man. I'm not going to say that Mormons are the most notorious penny pinchers out there, but they are certainly in the top five. (Insert your culturally insensitive joke here, because I certainly won't. Not that I'm not thinking it.)

Fighting Mormon moms for the chance at a cheap box of Rice-a-Roni proved to be eye opening. I saw what I looked like in the faces of other women. I stood in the background as they argued with cashiers, faces purple and spittle flying, carts filled with things they didn't need.

Our local Walmart decided they would incorporate a double coupon day on Tuesdays, and boy did they end up regretting it. By 9 p.m. on Monday nights, the store would be mobbed with women who knew what items they could get for nearly free with a doubled coupon. Carts would be loaded then babysat for hours, until midnight rolled around. At midnight, the hordes of crazy 'couponers' lined up and waited to get their free deals. It took me exactly one attempt at that nightmare to give up my dream of couponing in Utah.

After waiting in line for over an hour, it was my turn at the double couponing experience. The cashier was harried and resentful, and I was incredibly tired. It was nearly 1:30 a.m. and I was at Walmart! What world was I living in? Who was I and what had I done with the real Laura?

I stumbled through the handful of coupons I had, then loaded up and left, the echoes of other crazy women in my head. In the end, it was easy to quit. All I had to do was give up a few hours of sleep to realize that I value my sleep over a good deal. I value my antisocial shopping trips over the crowded Black Friday-like experiences of couponing. All in all, I'd rather have a supersized Diet Coke than fourteen boxes of hamburger helper. Life is good when you have your priorities straight.

My adventures in couponing lasted just over a year. By the year's end, I had enough toilet paper to last me over five years, more toothpaste than I could use in ten years, and only enough patience to use an occasional coupon at Burger King. I had made the decision to hang up my couponing cape, and to hand over the reins to those with more grit than I myself had.

To those of you still fighting the couponing battle, I wish you the very best. And be nice to those poor cashiers. You never know when they might snap.

Extreme Makeover Wingspan Edition

Several months ago, I bought a small suction cup that promised to get rid of cellulite. The infomercials promised huge changes! Amazing! A gorgeous (of course) woman took the small cup and, with a serene smile on her face, moved the cup up and down her (already smooth) thighs.

Next, they showed a before and after photo of the changes. It really was amazing! The difference was so pronounced I'm pretty sure the leg changed races! I was sold on the idea and bought the suction cup shortly after watching the commercial. My thighs, after all, are very Shirley Templesque—all dimples.

Two months passed, (shipping from China isn't fast, ya'll) and I finally received my cup in the mail. Ever ready for the ultimate thigh makeover, I ripped open the package and got to work.

The cup itself is made out of a silicone material, not unlike those pop-up toys in the shape of little bowls. I squeezed the cup together and stuck it on the most offensive part of my thigh, the inner upper. Ladies, you know what I mean. It is the part of the thigh that women want gone. The part that, if missing, creates the much envied 'thigh gap'. I don't know many normal women with a thigh gap. The only woman I know in real life with a gap literally has no stomach, and weighs 90 lbs. Even though only 0.01% of the population has a thigh gap, I don't know a woman out there who doesn't seek it.

I was determined to smooth away some of that thigh cottage cheese! I adopted a serene smile of my own and attempted to run the cup down my thigh. Only it would not budge. I pushed and pulled at it, while it stayed in place like a child's booger stuck to a wall.

Eventually, I was able to pull it off using Hercules like strength. I realized I would have a hickey the size of a dinner plate if I continued this way. I developed a strategy of putting lotion on my leg first, then pulling the cup up and down my thigh. I couldn't keep a straight face, because ya'll it hurt! The cup pulled my fat in directions it did not want to go. According to the infomercial, it was breaking up fat cells, and causing them to disperse. Where to, I don't know, but if I had to put money on it, I'd bet they settled in my brain.

No pain no gain, right? I continued this ritual nightly for an entire month, ready to see a new leg emerge from the depths of my fat encrusted old one.

I'm sure you'll be shocked to hear that my legs look just as cottage cheese like as before; if not more so. Surprise, surprise, the miracle suction cup didn't work. Neither did the tapeworm. Mostly because I didn't actually order it, though I mulled it over much longer than I probably should have.

I've written before on my weight loss journeys. Yes, I said journeys with an s. I'm consistently going up and down in weight. Usually up, but on a rare occasion I will become obsessed with a new diet and actually lose weight.

The last time I lost a significant amount of weight, I was following a fanatical plan, which helped me drop 75 pounds in less than a year. During that time, I was meaner than a rabid badger and sadder than an out of work clown. I was hungry, tired, and depressed at the thought of never eating candy again. But hey, I was thin!

The problem was, I was thin but not 'tight'. I had skin hanging down where my fat used to be. Like boobs after children, my skin sagged, unsupported by the fat that had once held it so nicely in place. No matter how many push-ups or thigh presses I did, I never could tone it up. When I would do yoga, I would watch my skin sag toward the floor in fascination. I didn't realize I had so much excess skin! If I were a bird, I would have a huge wingspan. No such luck, however. I am merely a human being. Wingspan doesn't amount to much.

I looked into farming out my excess skin for people needing skin grafts. Unfortunately, they don't accept skin from people like me. Alive, I mean. Most people get skin grafts from cadavers. Why someone would choose a dead body over this sexy one, I'll never know. But hey, if any of my dear readers are out there needing some live, extra, skin, I'm your gal.

Realizing I couldn't afford any plastic surgery, and my best efforts at filling the excess with muscle didn't seem to be working, I did the only logical thing left to do. I filled those empty spaces with fat. And boy, did that work quickly and, if I do say so myself, quite nicely.

Sure, I'm chunky again, but this time when I'm in downward dog pose, I don't sag. My fat is firm, and my pants are tight. Who cares if my muscles aren't?

P.E. and Me

Not long ago I subbed for a middle school P.E. teacher. I happened to sub for a class that had my 6th grade son in it, getting to see first-hand how my genetics played out. Watching those gangly preteens awkwardly run laps brought me back to my years in the Physical Education system. Seeing my son run with his arms swinging wildly at his sides brought back memories of my own attempts to run in P.E.

The highest point in my P.E. career was when I won the first-grade jump rope championship. I jumped consecutively longer than any other student in the first grade. So needless to say, I was a pretty big fucking deal. I got a yellow paper certificate that I still have today. While other people may have athletic trophies they proudly display, I have one crinkly certificate stating I could jump rope with the best of them in our small town elementary.

First grade was the height of my athletic prowess. It went downhill from there. I never again felt the high of winning, or even of being good at anything physical. I was inherently clumsy, and just lazy enough to not want to work hard at becoming better. When we had our annual physical exams, I would usually do poorly, below average at best.

My elementary P.E. teacher was a tall lanky woman with short, curly red hair. Her name was Ms Bus, and I recall being immensely disappointed that she wasn't as big as her name. She had played basketball in school and loved exercise. I imagined she was a huge fan of Jane Fonda videos and sweatbands. Out of all my P.E. teachers, she was my favorite. Probably because she had low expectations for elementary school students, which worked to my advantage. I would squeak by with barely passing scores, attempting to play the game smarter and not harder.

When we ran the mile in class, we followed the path of a baseball diamond near a grove of trees. We would run around and around, telling the teacher how many laps we had run each time we passed. I hadn't run more than two laps before I realized I could lag behind, sneak into the grove of trees, and come out at a later time.

I stopped, pretended to tie my shoe, then dove into the nearby bushes. I waited, searching to see if anyone noticed my deceit, then slowly inched back into the trees. I spent the next eight minutes poking things with sticks and watching other kids huff and puff, red faced, around and around like puppets; all the while snickering to myself at my evil genius.

Once the class had run all but one lap, I emerged to run with the class for the final lap. Because I was not in the finest of physical form, my face was just as red and sweaty as the rest of the class before I reached the final stopping place. Ms Bus looked at me, shook her head, and sighed. I could tell she was deciding whether or not to call me on my bullshit. Teaching a bunch of stupid kids must have taken its toll, because she didn't say anything. I may have felt a wave of guilt for making her question her career choice, but I determined it was worth it for getting out of twelve minutes of torture.

After graduating elementary school, I was in for a harsh reality check. Middle school was completely different, in all the wrong ways. It didn't help that my body was changing. I was in the process of 'becoming a woman' which meant I was struggling with weird half-boobs and diarrhoea causing menstrual cramps.

Adding to the fun of growing pains was the cold hard reality of taking showers after each P.E. class. Do you know what happens when you combine thirty preteen and teenaged girls with one shower head? A lot of body shaming. That's what. Taking off your clothes and washing your body in front of 29 other girls is a punishment reserved for the deepest circle of hell. Ya'll, it's really fucked up. Someone needs to be fired for that idiotic idea.

Our teacher's name was Ms Swift. Unlike Ms Bus, she was short and squat, with the physique of a wrestler. She took P.E. very seriously. If you were not 100% gung-ho about sit ups and softball, you were not on her good side. And if you had an 'attitude problem' about getting naked in front of everyone, you were on her shit list.

It was no surprise that I was on her list. The only time I enjoyed the showering rule was the day a spider crawled out of Krista Kerner's shorts, resulting in 29 shrill screams and the trampling stampede of a herd of girls.

Other than that, I dreaded it, often getting sent to the office for having a bad attitude. Ms Swift and I developed a hatred of each other that quickly turned into a battle of wills. She mocked me while I hung sadly on the chin up bar, unable to pull my beefy body up more than a quarter of an inch, and I mouthed off with regularity. All of that came to a head one day in 8th grade. That day I became infamous in the school.

The day before I had sprained my ankle (a common occurrence for me) so I didn't participate in the basketball games that were played that day, though I was forced to change into my P.E. clothes. After a relaxing period of sitting on the side-lines, I changed back into my regular clothes, only to hear one of my snitch-ass classmates yell, "Ms Swift, Laura isn't showering!"

I turned and shot the bitch a death glare, remembering her face, as she would be my enemy from that moment on. Ms Swift came out of her office and pointed a finger to the showers.

"Go shower." She held her arm out stiffly; this was her power play.

"I didn't play today."

"Doesn't matter," she countered. "Go shower."

I took a moment to fully absorb what she was saying. I hardened my resolve for fight for the right side of the matter.

"Why would I shower? I didn't do anything to get sweaty." I crossed my arms in defiance.

"It. Doesn't. Matter." She growled it out between her teeth. "Go shower."

"No."

The class was silent, collectively holding their breath. It wasn't often a student didn't back down. But this time I knew I was right. There was no reason for me to shower. Either she just wanted to see my naked body, or she was trying to assert dominance. Either way, I found it unacceptable.

"Get in the shower right now!" Her voice rose higher, and I knew I had to get out of there quickly.

"You can't make me, and I won't do it!" I yelled, pushing past her to run out the door. She grabbed at my shirt and I heard a tearing sound. Knowing she had ripped my favorite shirt, I took off, stomping gorilla-like through the hallways. She came after me, yelling my name.

"Laura, get back here right now!"

I stormed past the study hall, ignoring all the student's eyes on me, knowing they were listening to the verbal telling off I was receiving.

"Go to the office!" Realizing people could see me disobeying her orders, Ms Swift changed her tune. No longer did she expect me to stop, but to go straight to the principal's office. Instead, I headed for the front door of the school. I didn't know what the plan would be after I walked out, but I had every intention of marching right through the door.

The moment I got to the front door, the principal, a 6' 8" mammoth of a man, grabbed me by the collar and pulled me into his office. I spent the rest of the day in detention and the next two days suspended. I was grounded for a month and received quite a tongue lashing from my dad; but I couldn't help but feel it was worth it. I had held my ground against unrighteous tyranny.

Thankfully, Ms Swift and I eventually learned to tolerate each other. I survived field hockey and wrestling, and she tolerated my toned down 'tude. When I moved on to high school, we both breathed a sigh of relief.

Ms Halliday was my high school teacher, and we had a relationship where we happily ignored one another. Other than the occasional class skipping and ass scratching instead of running, I wasn't too bad to be around. I got decent grades and muddled my way through. Part of it must have been maturity, because I knew that if I could just hold on long enough, I would be free. And I would have done anything to get out of P.E. for the rest of my life.

Because God help us all if we were forced to be active the rest of our lives, am I right? We might actually live longer. And what kind of sicko wants that?

Six Times Six Equals Thirty-Six I Think

I don't know what kind of hash my teachers were smoking in my small-town elementary school, but it must have been pretty strong the day they came up with how to teach us multiplication. While I was never great at math to begin with, often sweating more than working during our 'timed' tests, I did even worse after attempting to learn something these geniuses called 'sound multiplication'.

To this day, I have never been able to find the program they used. It must have been experimental, and I'm guessing there were so many complaints they buried it deep. But not until they ruined my entire mathematical future. Sure, it seems I wasn't given any God-given math talents, but who could say what NASA career I missed out on because of this educational faux-pas?

The concept was this: assign each number a sound, then combine the two sounds together. These sounds would equal a picture, and that picture would correspond with an answer. For example, the number six is associated with the sound 'ch'. So six, or 'ch' times six, is 'ch ch'. 'Ch ch' creates the picture of a train, because trains make the sound 'choo choo'. The train is associated with the number 36. Therefore, 6 times 6 is 36. Easy right?

Fuck no. It was not easy. Not at all. You know what is easy? What the rest of the world does: memorizing the multiplication chart. Instead of simplifying the process, the staff at Kluckholn Elementary decided to add in multiple steps, for no other apparent reason than watching a bunch of fourth graders attempt to sound out math like drunken German squirrels. Or perhaps they got a sick satisfaction out of knowing that this group of kids would never grow up to amount to anything worth a lick mathematically. Whatever the reason, it was a really shitty thing to do. To this day, the only thing I remember is six times six. It equals 36. I think.

Stumbling through math my entire life, it was easy to blame my lack of skill on those teachers. They were the stepping stone to my consistently terrible arithmetic grades; at least in my mind. In middle school, I somehow plunked through with Ds, never quite failing, but always one sneeze away from it. I cheated, writing answers on my arms, hands, feet—whatever I thought I could possibly get away with. I peeked at other people's papers and attempted to see the reflection of answers off the kid's glasses from across the room. I refused to work harder, just smarter. Or lazier. Tomato, tah-mah-toe.

Cheating got me through math (barely) until college. I chose a major knowing full well there would be as little math as possible within it. Unfortunately, there were still general math requirements, as well as a statistics class. In these classes, you were required to get at least a C in order to pass. Easy, right? Maybe, if you could, at bare minimum, understand your professor's language.

My first statistics teacher, Professor Kim, was straight out of Korea. He was incredibly smart, but for the life of me I could not understand a damn thing he said. His accent was so thick I could not decipher 10 out of 15 words he spoke. It didn't help that in addition to his accent he was speaking a different language: statistics.

I find statistics fascinating to read, but terrifyingly frustrating to compute. I never appreciated algebra, with its various possibilities for x and y, so it was hard to enjoy doing more of it for college credit. While the students around me quickly typed numbers into their fancy calculators, I daydreamed about how I could pass this class without any effort on my part.

I attended class for two weeks before I succumbed to my true nature and just gave up. Being the idiot I was (am), I didn't drop the class, I just failed it by non-attendance. This led to a big fat F, bringing my otherwise excellent GPA down. I would have gladly taken the lowered GPA if it meant I didn't have to take the class again. But alas, I did.

I started the second time around with a better attitude and a professor I could understand. When he had us introduce ourselves, (a process I hate by the way) I introduced myself by saying I was taking the class for the second time, and I needed all the help I could get. The class laughed, but I was dead serious.

My strategy for passing was a combination of minimal effort, medium cheating, and maximum pity from the professor. I figured if I could balance all three, I could manage a C. Being as slow as I am, playing dumb was no act. I felt the pity rise each time I attempted to answer a question, the room full of cringes and awkward coughs.

On pop quizzes, I relied on the small amount of formulas I recalled from my homework, and sneaking peaks at the papers next to mine, all the while praying to the god of cheaters and goons that my efforts would be enough. Usually they resulted in Ds and Fs, so I guess the answer was no.

My homework brought my average in the class up, mostly because I wasn't doing it. Someone else was. (Here is where my fiancé points out that I didn't understand anything because I wasn't doing anything. I would like to point out that he can shut it.) I was dating a math wizard at the time, and often he would do my math homework for me while I was busy taking a nap. This left me with (obviously) unearned but good homework scores, and terrible testing scores. I told the professor I was bad at testing, (which is true, but I'm also bad at everything else, so…) and he kindly offered me more time or a quieter environment to take the quizzes. I'm guessing he knew I would decline, seeing as how my only hope at passing was the smart kid next to me. If you catch my drift…wink wink.

Cheating during math was difficult when they required you to show your work, which was always! I marvelled at the kid in class who would be irritated with showing his work because he could come up with the answer in his head. I, the person who still does addition on scrap paper, (not to mention my fingers) hated showing my work because I had no idea how the person I was cheating off got their answer. It all looked like gobbledygook to me. When forced to show my work, I often used a combination of terrible handwriting and scribbles to disguise the fact that my 'work' looked like the nonsensical musings of a madwoman. Which it was. It was:

nonsense plus nonsense divided by nonsense equals correct answer. In that order.

Eventually I came to the end of the semester, and was skirting a C, thanks to the homework unethically gained via boyfriend. The final exam was 40% of our grade, and I knew I would fail it. I developed a back-up plan, based on the pity portion of my strategy.

I wrote an essay, attempting to amuse the professor so much he couldn't help but to give me a C. My essay was titled 'Why You Should Pass Laura', and included such hilarious reasons as, if you don't, her blood will be on your hands because she will kill herself, and, if she doesn't pass, she will never get out of college, and will die homeless in a box under an overpass. Then, after botching my final exam, I turned my essay in with flair, crossing my fingers that it might spark some sympathy within this peculiar man who taught math for a living.

It worked. Truthfully, it is possible my average rounded up to a C, but I wouldn't know because I suck at math. But more likely, my professor fudged the numbers and helped me out. Whether it was because he thought I was funny, or because he didn't want to deal with me another semester, I will never know. I don't care what the reason is, only that it happened. And that this professor, even though I can't recall his name, taught me more about how to pass a math class than my fourth-grade teacher ever could.

To Stay at Home or Not? That is the Question

Growing up Mormon is tricky when you're a female. There is a definite difference in roles between the men and the women in the church. Generally, men are told to be the breadwinners and sole providers for the family, while the women are encouraged to stay home and nurture the family. I know, barf, right?

Being a girl, I was brought up in the church with those goals in mind. Luckily, my parents were cool, and I never got the feeling they would be sad if I chose to work outside the home, or if I never got married or had children. In hindsight, they were probably prematurely afraid for any husband or kids I may have. But groomed to be a stay-at-home-mom I was!

I went to college (Mormons also value education for both males and females, which is very progressive of them considering), and graduated on the Dean's Honour roll, with Bachelor of Science degrees in Sociology, Human Development and Family Studies, and Criminology and Corrections (with a minor in Psychology). What can I say, I was an overachiever with big dreams.

Halfway through my college career, I served a mission for my church in Sydney Australia. This alone went against the norm for Mormon women. Most females within the church don't serve missions, as they are (or were) considered to be unattractive if they weren't married before missionary age. Age 21. Things have changed slightly, but when I served a mission there were definite stereotypes. The boys who served were obedient and stalwart sons of God. The girls were old hags, single and miserable, probably guilty of having multiple facial warts and nothing else to do with their time.

After my mission, I began dating and eventually married. One month after getting married, I got pregnant. I was, at the time, on birth control. I took the pregnancy to mean that it was God's will. Everything, as a faithful Mormon, is God's will.

I finished up college and graduated in my 6th month of pregnancy. I spent the next few months getting rejected for positions because I was pregnant. Regardless of what the law says, no one wants to hire a pregnant lady, especially in Utah, where I resided at the time. Whether or not they would admit it, Mormon employers felt my place was in the home, and that I would (and should) stay there once the baby was born.

My son was born, followed by a daughter 20 months later. One day after she was born, my divorce was final, and I found myself a single mom. I struggled to find a place to live, a way to finance it, and food to eat. I had two babies under two, and I was not loving it. I loved my children, but I did not love the welfare I had to use. This is why after only a one-year divorce, I got back together with my ex-husband for a second chance at an 'eternal family' (another Mormon concept).

We squeezed the bulbous pimple that was our marriage for almost ten years; attempting to make that marriage work.

During those ten years, I was a bonafide stay-at-home-mom. I did everything except earn the money. I cooked, cleaned, took care of the children, and rarely left the home for anything unrelated to the job of mom. It was gruelling, but I enjoyed most of it. What I didn't enjoy was the judgement of those who thought it wasn't 'real work'.

Having been both a stay-at-home-mom and a working mother, I can honestly say there are different challenges associated with both. For me, the biggest challenge of staying at home was the feeling of being unnoticed and unappreciated. I felt invisible, like if I were to disappear, no one would notice, and probably not even care. Sure, my kids would wonder where their personal slave went, and my husband would have to find another hole to plough, but other than that, I was merely a blip in the universe that was my life. Even I wouldn't miss me, because I wasn't even sure who or what I was anymore. My life was so fully enmeshed with my family, I didn't know where I began or ended. It was depressing.

Once the kids were in school all day, I started searching for work. This was a struggle in and of itself, because even though I had multiple degrees gathering dust on my wall, I hadn't had a 'real job' in almost a decade. Eventually someone seemed desperate enough to take a chance on me and I began 'working' again.

As a working mom (I hate this term by the way, don't ask me why), I discovered again who I was and what I enjoyed doing outside of the home. I got to participate in actual adult conversations and feel appreciated for my work. Best of all, I got paid!

But I missed a lot when I was away. I missed class parties and performances and having snacks and hugs ready for the kids when they got home from school. I missed having the energy for bike rides and puzzles and night-time cuddles. The guilt for missing those things hits moms particularly hard. Somehow, I doubt men feel it as acutely as women.

Out of the home, the judgement switches from 'How can you leave your babies to work outside the home?' to 'Don't you want to make a difference in the world and do something bigger than be a mom?' Either you are stuck with the judgmental stay-at-home-Nazis, or the judgmental work-outside-the-home ones. You can't win either way. Unless, of course, you are a man.

Men get to choose so much in this life. The feminist in me wants to take to the street and protest. The couch potato in me would rather write about it while eating Funyuns. I couldn't help being bitter in my Mormon marriage, knowing that I had so little choice in what I could do within the confines of our own family.

My path has taken me away from such a rigorous religion, though the rest of my family is entrenched in it. Because they are happy within it, I am happy for them. I also know that I am happier outside of it, and even more ecstatic to be outside of my unhappy marriage.

I couldn't tell you one way or another if I like working outside the home or within it more. I can say, however, that as a woman, I have the back of my sisters and support their choices; no judgement here.

Bitches Be Trippin'

September 16th, 2011 is a day that will go down in history as one that changed my life completely. Every day since that has been affected, and every step made more painful. Think I'm being dramatic? Let me walk you (painfully) through it.

It started simply enough. I was scammed (damn it, Laura) into a 'free' weekend getaway at a resort in Park City, Utah. When I say scammed, I mean when I agreed to take the free weekend, I didn't know that you were forced to sit in a time share presentation for several hours in order for it to be free. Sadly, this is not the only time I have thusly been fooled. But more on that later.

My husband (now ex) and I headed up there, telling ourselves we could get past the whole 'overbearing pressure' of the timeshare deal, and enjoy the weekend. My parents agreed to watch the kids for the first night, after which we would pick them up and enjoy the second day and night together as a cosy little family.

At this point in our marriage, we were five and a half years in, the magic somewhat (okay, totally) faded, tarnished by children and hearing each other expel various bodily fluids. I figured I could bring some romance back into the equation with some ill-fitting lingerie and a 'sex game' I bought at some store that promised to bring the flame back into your love life.

After a romantic dinner of Taco Bell, we went swimming, lounged in the hot tub, and headed back to our room. I squeezed myself into my newly purchased get up, looking like a sausage spilling out of its casing.

We began the game. It was a truth or dare kind of game, only with the dares supplied. I was relieved, because my go to dares would have gotten us arrested. Running around the facility in your underwear is less accepted as a dare when you are an adult.

Both of us were horrible at this game. The very first question demanded we role play. Outside of theatre class, I did not enjoy role play. I found it difficult to pretend to be a naughty French maid, or a teacher scolding a student. In both scenarios, I couldn't help but think, *Wait! This can only lead to me losing my job and getting arrested! I've got floors to clean or classes to teach! I don't have time for these shenanigans.* I was not good at this.

Eventually the game was discarded, and we watched something on TV. My guess is we watched something he enjoyed, and I tolerated. A perfect parallel of our marriage. We fell asleep, and spent the night tossing and turning, unaccustomed to such a nice mattress, and no annoying children.

The next morning, we got ready to go and pick up the kids. I was excited to take them around the property, and to get out of the oppressive 'just me and him' atmosphere. I grabbed my cup from the previous evening, remembering that refills of my beloved Diet Coke were only 75 cents if you brought in your same cup. For some incredibly sad reason, this was one of the most exciting parts of the trip. Cheap Diet Coke? I'd sit through a four-hour, high-stress presentation for that!

We headed out, my cup in hand, ready to get caffeine and start the day right. Instead, as we headed down the stairs, my life changed. In typical Laura fashion.

Going down the multiple steps on my Diet Coke quest, I landed hard on the last one. I heard an unmistakable pop, lost my balance, caught myself with my other leg, then went down hard. I looked down, only to see my right ankle was attempting to exit the confines of my skin. At this point, I groaned, noticing I had dropped my cup in the mud. *There go my cheap refills*, I thought. Followed quickly with, *Holy shit! The pain!* Then, *Yes! I bet they won't make us go to the timeshare presentation now!*

My husband, who had been several feet ahead of me, looked back, finally realizing I wasn't right behind him. He came over, shaking his head at my clumsiness. When he got close enough to see my ankle's misfortune, he held out his hands like a confident surgeon.

"You just need to pop it back into place," he said, his fingers inching closer to my leg.

"Don't you touch me!" I squealed, perhaps too loudly for so early in the morning.

"Call 911," I implored, tears of pain starting to roll down my cheeks.

"That will cost a fortune. I'll help you to the car." I stared hard at him, anger and vomit bitter in my throat. I looked at my other ankle, already almost as swollen as the dislocated one.

"I can't walk like this," I cried, realizing someone was going to have to put me on a stretcher.

After haggling for a few more minutes, he started to get embarrassed at how desperate I was sounding. I think I even called out for help to a passer-by. Fearing people would start to think he had pushed me, he finally called 911.

After lying in the mud for what seemed like forever, the paramedics came. I noticed only then that the skirt I had been wearing was up to my waist, and they were getting an eyeful of whatever old lady panties I had donned that morning. I struggled to pull my skirt down, gasping as they tried to stabilize my leg.

While I was being loaded on a stretcher, I told my husband to call my mom. He finally did, and I think I heard her chuckling. "She just twisted her ankle," he said into the phone. It was then I knew I would stab him if only the paramedics would roll me close enough. Instead, they loaded me into the ambulance, and pumped me full of morphine. Would they do that just for a twisted ankle? I think not.

I remember the two-million-dollar ambulance ride to the hospital, trying to make small talk with the paramedic, who I felt hated me. I sensed he was disappointed with me, wishing for a bullet riddled victim instead of a harpooned whale like woman.

We got to the E.R., and I was gratified to see people taking my injury seriously; doctors and nurses milling about like I was someone important. I might have revelled in the attention, if I had known it was due to something other than my clumsiness. I assumed they were shaking their heads thinking, "How could someone get so injured by walking down the stairs? What an idiot."

After a few X-rays (and an embarrassing situation in which they cut me out of my underwear), they determined they needed to set the bone and relocate the ankle joint. Duh. They also determined that I needed to be semiconscious for this. They were afraid if they completely knocked me out, I'd vomit my breakfast muffin up, then choke to death on it. At that point, I wanted to take the chance.

Despite my pleas, they gave me something that they said would numb the pain and set to work. I remember bits and pieces, as I was trippin' balls, high on some sort of LSD like drug. Or maybe it was LSD. Either way, it was crazy!

I'm pretty sure that my 'essence' was floating all around the room, while my body laid there suffering. I heard people talking, orders being given, and a sound, somewhat like a walrus being stepped on. "Uhhhhhh!" I heard it go. "Uuuuhhhhhhhh!"

At some point in my floating adventure, I realized the walrus was me. I was making those sounds every time someone would move either of my legs. *Oh my*, I thought, *that is an unattractive noise.* But I couldn't help it, so walrus mewing I did, until they stopped treating me like a Claymation project.

"It will probably be a long time before she comes out of it," I heard the doctor tell my husband. *I'll show you*, I thought, then tried my best to will myself back down from my drug induced trip.

I forced myself to open my eyes and began the journey of letting the doctors know I'd been stuck on a wooden stretcher for multiple hours, and my butt hurt more than either of my legs did. They removed the stretcher and told me I had a severe sprain in my left leg and ankle, and my right ankle was dislocated, with multiple (four) breaks in the leg and ankle. I would need multiple surgeries. I remember being somewhat smug that my husband was wrong with his 'twisted ankle' assessment. Dumbass.

I was wheeled into a hospital room, knowing I would have surgery the next day. Here I would spend some of the most humiliating times of my life. And it all started with my epic bladder.

I've written about my ability to hold bathtub amounts of pee, so it's no surprise that my amount of urine would be the cause of so much humiliation. But alas, it was.

The nurses had the terrible job of trying to wedge a bedpan under my manatee carcass each and every time I had to pee. And with all the fluids they were pumping into me, I had to pee a lot. Because I couldn't lift my body weight with my legs, nor could I walk anywhere, the bedpan was my only option, since they were being stingy with the catheter. I've said it before and I'll say it again: I want to be able to pee whenever and wherever I want. Fuck the 'increased risk of infection'.

We'd go through the same carefully coordinated back and forth motion, trying to get enough momentum to slide the bedpan under my blubber as I rocked forward. Then, once it was in place, I would relieve myself, only to overflow the pan. Humiliated, I would begin to cry as the CNA had to clean it up, muttering to herself each time.

After two times of this, I began to stop peeing about half way through. I'd tell them I still had to go, and we'd rock again, so I could finish. This worked like a charm, and I was quite proud of myself, until the stress of my weight broke the bedpan!

In my defence, it was a flimsy plastic bedpan that had probably seen better days. However, you do not know complete and utter humiliation until your fat ass has obliterated a pan designed to endure bodyweight on top of it. To this day, I still cringe when I think of it.

The day after my fateful trip down the stairs (no pun intended), I was wheeled down to surgery. They told me that my injury was so bad, they could not perform the originally planned surgery (to add screws and plates to the bones) and would instead need to place an external fixator.

This is a psychologically scarring procedure. For nearly two weeks, I laid in bed staring at multiple metal rods sticking out of my leg. Just knowing that each metal rod was screwed into my bones gave me the shivers. I dealt with that until the swelling went down enough to have 12 screws and two metal plates inserted.

Over the next few years I had multiple surgeries and dozens and dozens of trips to physical therapy. I had muscles lengthened, and hardware removed, since it was removing itself whether I like it or not. I got to have a handicapped tag for my car, and to ride on the little scooters at Walmart. I had to have sponge baths for way too long, and leg hair unlike anything you've ever seen.

I was told after my last surgery and accompanying physical therapy that there was nothing more they could do for me. Eventually, I'd need to get a complete ankle replacement, but they wouldn't recommend that until the pain became unbearable. It would seem that ankle joints are quite finicky, and that replacements of them are somewhat new.

I limp, each and every day. I wake up and stumble around like a zombie, and hobble to and fro until my ankle decides both warm up and chill the fuck out. I grit my teeth when I step weird, or when my leg aches in the cold. It's no fun, this stupid injury.

My pride has been affected along with my mobility. Things that were once second nature, like squatting, I can no longer do. I can't run, but instead I have to skip like a schoolgirl anytime I'm in a hurry. Oh, little Timmy fell down the well! Why the hell is that lady skipping to the rescue? What an insensitive bitch; skipping at a time like this.

My kids know they can always run away from me, and that short of a tasing, they can easily out maneuver any attempted physical punishment. My jobs have been affected, along with my for-fun activities. I can no longer skate, ski, or even jump on a trampoline. Not that I ever did any of this to begin with. But I might have started, you never know. According to my orthopaedic surgeon (ever the ray of sunshine), every step I take is causing more damage to my ankle, and I soon might as well be dead.

I have no cartilage in my ankle. Each movement scrapes bone against bone, the physical equivalent of Fran Drescher's laugh. But it is humbling, and, like my dad always used to say, it gives me something to complain about. So, I've got that going for me.

I suppose the moral of the story is this: If you want to get out of a timeshare presentation, horribly injure yourself. Just beware, you may miss out on those cheap Diet Coke refills.

Third Time is the Charm I hope

I'm about to get married for the 3rd time. I told myself after my second divorce I would never get married again. No way, no how. It would seem I am terrible at it. The reasoning behind my anti-third marriage stance wasn't that I have a problem with marriage, just that I have a hatred of divorce. The expense, the fighting, the bad feelings all around. Gross. There is also the fact that I have very little hope that lasting and true love even exists. Does anyone even know how to love? Can unconditional love ever truly happen? All these questions rattle around in my brain when contemplating marriage.

As if I didn't need another reason to not want a third marriage, the never-ending planning of weddings and receptions and showers and parties makes me tired just thinking about it. The stress that goes along with all of it never seemed worth it to me. But alas, here I am again.

My original idea was to make my fiancé plan the entire wedding while I sat back and relaxed. Soon after, I remembered if I let him plan it, it would never happen. Ordinarily I wouldn't care, but since he is the perfect man, I want to lock that booty down quick before he goes and changes his mind. Which is also why instead of waiting for him to propose, I went and did it myself. Was it romantic? Not really. It wasn't even that creative. But I got down on one knee like a baller and asked him to be mine.

Nothing about our relationship is all that conventional. I am 11 years older, I've been married and divorced twice, and have two kids saddled at my side. Even though he knew my age and my history, he still asked me to be his girlfriend, which shocked me so much he had to repeat himself (twice, he points out) to get an answer. To be honest, I wasn't even aware people asked each other out anymore. I was under the impression everyone just had casual sexual relationships then moved on to other casual relationships.

Now that I am planning to get married again, I'm trying to rid myself of the conventional idea that it's the bride and groom's job to make everyone happy. Attempting to do so is the worst and most stressful part of planning a wedding.

Unfortunately, most weddings aren't really for the bride and groom. They are for the mother, the mother-in-law, the brothers and sisters, the aunts and uncles. Even the dogs of family members are taken into account when focusing on everyone else. The act of trying to please people is what makes a bride so miserable while she is planning the wedding, and sometimes even during it. Having been married twice before, I can't say I blame women when their inner bridezilla comes out.

My first wedding nearly killed me; my attempts at trying to save my parents money nearly drove me to call it all off. If I had known what my other siblings would spend, I wouldn't have bothered. Ever the frugal consumer, I haggled over the prices of bouquets, dresses, and catering. I determined it would be cheaper to hold the reception in my parents' backyard, forgetting that we would have to put in hours of work to make it 'reception worthy'. Yard work is my seventh circle of hell, but hey it saved a few bucks.

When the day of my wedding finally arrived, I was a complete and utter mess. Adding to my stress was the fact that I was no longer worthy to be married in the Mormon temple. Mormons have a lot of strict rules on who can get married in their temples. You must pass a worthiness interview to even enter the temple, much less get married there. Non-members of The Church of Jesus Christ of Latter-Day Saints are not even allowed within the walls other than in a designated waiting room. Members themselves are allowed only if the can satisfactorily answer the following:

1. Do you have faith in and a testimony of God the Eternal Father, His Son Jesus Christ, and the Holy Ghost?
2. Do you have a testimony of the Atonement of Christ and of His role as Saviour and Redeemer?
3. Do you have a testimony of the restoration of the gospel in these the latter days?
4. Do you sustain the President of the Church of Jesus Christ of Latter-Day Saints as the Prophet, Seer, and Revelator and as the only person on the earth who possesses and is authorized to exercise all priesthood keys? Do you sustain members of the First Presidency and the Quorum of the Twelve Apostles as prophets, seers, and revelators? Do you sustain the other General Authorities and local authorities of the Church?
5. Do you live the law of chastity?

6. Is there anything in your conduct relating to members of your family that is not in harmony with the teachings of the Church?
7. Do you support, affiliate with, or agree with any group or individual whose teachings or practices are contrary to or oppose those accepted by the Church of Jesus Christ of Latter-Day Saints?
8. Do you strive to keep the covenants you have made, to attend your sacrament and other meetings, and to keep your life in harmony with the laws and commandments of the gospel?
9. Are you honest in your dealings with your fellow men?
10. Are you a full-tithe payer?
11. Do your keep the Word of Wisdom?
12. Do you have financial or other obligations to a former spouse or children? If yes, are you current in meeting those obligations?
13. If you have previously received your temple endowment: 1) Do you keep the covenants that you made in the temple? 2) Do you wear the garment both night and day as instructed in the endowment and in accordance with the covenant you made in the temple?
14. Have there been any sins or misdeeds in your life that should have been resolved with priesthood authorities but have not been?
15. Do you consider yourself worthy to enter the Lord's house and participate in temple ordinances?

As for me, I could answer most of these with sincerity, except for the one about keeping the law of chastity. For those of you that have no idea what that means, take heart, I'm about to tell you. In a nutshell, to obey the law of chastity means you haven't smashed boots, scrubbed, or even lightly polished them with anyone else. Namely, you have not had any sexual relations with a person outside of the marriage covenant. This I lied about, because: spoiler alert, I had. Therefore, I couldn't in good faith be married in the temple. But the shame placed upon couples who are not married in the temple seemed insurmountable to me. So, I lied.

To be honest, I feel really bad for Mormons. They are expected to abstain from any sexual contact until after they are married. While I certainly understand the reasoning behind this, I also question if whether this is the most practical thing to do. (Even as I write this I laugh, because when has religion ever been practical?) Sexual incompatibility can be a huge problem in relationships, and it seems like a good idea to nip those problems in the bud by sampling the goods before you buy. What if 'things' don't fit like you hoped they would? What if your significant other has more parts than you had originally bargained on? Wouldn't you want to know beforehand? This is just my two cents, and definitely not what the church teaches. I guess they advocate the element of surprise.

For me, I had a moment of weakness in which I sampled the goods and lost my virgin status. So, when entering the temple, I knew I was not worthy, and it weighed on my heart. By the time I had stepped foot inside, I was positive God was going to strike me down at any moment. I nearly had a breakdown and spent several minutes in tears. The guilt was awful and ruined not only what was supposed to be the happiest moment of my life but convinced me for nearly a decade after that my transgression was the reason my marriage had failed.

In Mormon Temple weddings, you are not allowed to wear a dress without full length sleeves, the neckline up to the collar, and the length down to your feet. Even if you have a dress that hits all those requirements, it is covered for the majority of the time by various religious garb. You don't get that romantic walk down the aisle portrayed in movies, or even the pretty music. It can be incredibly disappointing for those looking for a magical moment, and my first wedding there in the temple was anything but magical.

My second wedding was just a trip to the courthouse. Easy, peasy. No fuss, no muss, and I didn't even dress up. Instead of a bouquet, I was carrying an extra 30 pounds from my daughter's birth the year before. It was the least romantic event ever, and I was okay with it. I had already had my 'wedding', and I didn't need or want another one. Upon my second divorce, I was even more determined to never get married again. But then I met my fiancé, and things changed, as they so annoyingly do.

My strategy this time is to please me and my fiancé only. If other people enjoy themselves, good. If not, I can't say that I give a damn. Because it is my fiancé's first (and hopefully last) wedding, I want him to be happy. Magnanimous woman that I am, I've told him he can take the lead in planning. But because he is a man and doesn't really care about the details, I'm doing most of it anyway.

In just a few months, I will walk down an aisle, in a beautiful dress, to the man I actually know I want to spend forever with. We are spending money on what we want to and ignoring the rest. Other than a small remembrance gift, the guests will receive only the joy of being invited to our wedding, which should be enough. There will be no reception, no cake, and no added expense. And ladies and gentlemen, I am really, truly, excited.

Final Destination: Hell

I really hate flying. It isn't so much the actual flying through the air that I can't stand, I just hate the entire process. Getting there, fighting to figure out how to navigate an airport so large it has its own zip code, and then getting dropped off at the designated drop off, which you may not, under any circumstances, get confused with the arrivals section. If you do, you will get honked at and yelled at by everyone from bus drivers to the security patrolling the area.

Once in the airport, you will stand in an absurdly long line in order to get your stuff torn through and your body mauled and ogled at by TSA agents with nothing better to do.

I usually make it to the airport just fine. Security is where I seem to always get caught up in something foul. I've had Christmas gifts opened, candy swabbed for explosives, and granny undies pulled out and unfolded for all to see.

The last time I was traveling, I had an entire bag of goodies packed to share with my children and my nieces and nephews once we got to our final destination. It was easily ten pounds of candy. Suckers, mini chocolate bars, and a few bags of Cheetos. My typically rotten luck assigned us an over-enthusiastic TSA agent who decided to hold up the line by taking out each and every candy item and swabbing it for explosives. My kids and I stood there, looking like fat asses, while other people shook their heads at my parenting.

"And this is just for the three-hour flight!" I announced to anyone who would listen. The TSA agent began to finger my opened bag of Cheetos.

"At least buy me dinner first," I cracked, hoping to ease the tension. It didn't work, and people behind me began to grumble and angrily shuffle their feet; the only thing you can do in an airport these days to vent your frustration. Make any loud complaint and before you know it, you'll be carted off in handcuffs to a scary back room, never to be seen again.

Eventually our agent cleared us to pass and we skulked off, red faced and fat shamed. I vowed to never bring candy with me again, but surprise, surprise, I've got a bag full of it today.

This time the candy wasn't even an issue. They didn't even look at it. Go figure. Today they were more interested in, as the TSA agent called it, my (insert hand waving at my crotch region here). The TSA agent ordered me to take things out of my pockets, rolling her eyes that I hadn't followed directions the first time. I assured her I was an obedient traveller and had nothing in my pockets.

"Well," she snidely remarked, "the machine says you have something in your pants."

My inner monologue went something like this: *Laura, don't say, 'just dis dick'. She won't think it is funny*. My outer dialogue said, "Just dis dick." Because I never listen to my brain. The heart wants what it wants, regardless of what the brain knows.

"Ma'am, do you want to have a private screening?" I'm sure it wasn't a veiled threat, but it sure sounded like one.

"No," I sighed, "we can do it here."

She commenced manhandling me, telling me to 'create a wider stance' when my legs weren't spread far apart enough for a small nation to enter. I attempted to go to my happy place while her hands went up and down my legs, though her command to 'keep my arms up' kept dragging me back down to the cold reality of traveling in today's world.

Once again, I made it past security, put my shoes back on, and lumbered to the gate. Getting on the airplane can be a nightmare of 'Lord of the Flies' proportions. Passengers passive-aggressively inch closer to the boarding gate, daring anyone to step in front of them. Everyone eyes each other looking for small seat kicking children, and fat people; searching for the few seatmates they might consider acceptable to sit by. I stopped playing the guessing game after I got 100% of the people I did not want to sit by as seatmates. I think the game is rigged.

But today is different. It may be the best day of my life, because I get to sit in first class. I've sat in first class only one other time in my life, and it was a disaster. I was flying to Florida and had been excited about it for days. Yes, I was excited for the cruise and for the Bahamas, but I was extra excited to sit with the bigwigs up at the front of the plane. I desperately wanted everyone's envying eyes upon me as I boarded first. I wanted that big seat for my fat ass and I wanted a warm cookie and hot towel. I resisted the urge to wave my ticket around in the faces of my lessers and boarded the plane with my dignity intact. However, when I got to my seat (the first one on the plane), someone was already sitting in it.

"Oh," I stammered politely, "I think you may be in my seat."

The man in my chair barely gave me a glance and waved to a seat a few rows back.

"Yeah you can take my seat." I stood, uncertain as to what to do, for a fraction of a second. When I didn't move, he took out his earbuds and stood up, facing me aggressively.

"I want to sit by my son. So unless you just need to sit by him for some reason, you can switch seats with me. It is still in first class, so I don't know what your problem is."

I stared at his teenage son for a moment, mouth agape at this man's rudeness. And, because I am never one to start a scene, I walked down the rows and sat in his empty seat. Up ahead I saw him turn to the woman behind him.

"The nerve of people!" I heard him announce to her. "I mean, I wasn't asking for much! Just to sit by my child!" The woman nodded and glared at me.

What the hell? I remember thinking. What did I do? I didn't even say anything! And would it have killed him to just politely ask instead of demand? I would have switched with him if he had asked nicely. What was his problem?

Though the flight was pleasant enough, I spent it in a foul mood, wishing overhead items would fall on him, or some crazy malfunction would decapitate him. I had been looking forward to this for weeks, and this fucker had ruined it for me. I stewed about something most people would merely brush off for weeks. I've never been good at letting stupid shit go.

Today my experience is all good up here in first class. I have eaten a cheese plate, and the fabulous flight attendant Andrew has been consistently refilling my diet coke. My legs are stretched out and there are no fart smells wafting back from any passengers in front of me. I have a special bathroom to use if I need to, and I even have a blanket I'm contemplating stealing for my cats. Really, I don't know how anyone travels any other way.

I'm going to be really disappointed on the flight home, stuck in coach, squashed between a sumo wrestler and a crying baby, with a brat behind me kicking my seat. I'll be missing this—a time when the only farts I could smell wafting back were my own.

Hoarders: Operation Laura

Ya'll, I am obsessed with shows about hoarders. While I am not someone who loves to binge watch TV, I could spend days munching on popcorn and watching shows about people who collect garbage. These shows are like crack to me.

There is something about watching people with mountains of garbage in their home that makes me feel better about my life. I'll sit there and think, *I may not fit into my pants, but at least I don't have stacks of feces-filled adult diapers up to the ceiling. I'm winning at life!* Low standards be damned.

Rumour has it that my great-grandmother on my dad's side was a hoarder. My dad would tell us that she had so much stuff jammed in her home, there were merely small pathways where there should have been rooms. He recalled that he and his siblings came across cases of bottled fruit so old they called it 'Dr Kevorkian juice'. Stories like this delight me. I love the idea of mountains of junk. This makes every bare spot like a secret hideaway in your own home!

Sadly, my great-grandma died before I was born, resulting in me never getting the opportunity to explore the caverns of her hoard. Dad always said we would have gotten along wonderfully, since we have very similar personalities.

"Quirky," he would call it. In truth, he probably thought I had the propensity to become a hoarder of epic proportions.

As a child, I was an avid collector. Obsessive, if you will. If there were 'collectable' toys on the market, I did my best to make sure I had each and every one. I wasn't satisfied if my collection wasn't complete. I had massive piles of My Little Ponies and Barbies scattering my room. I wanted them all.

I also assigned feelings and emotions to my belongings. This is apparently step one in 'how to become a hoarder'. Unable to avoid it, I had to sleep with every single pillow, blanket, and stuffed animal, so none of their 'feelings' got hurt. Heaven forbid a pillow get resentful that I didn't use it one night. "That bitch!" I imagined it saying, "She thinks she's too good for me. Well one day some other pillow is going to tell her she has an abnormally bulbous and heavy head. Then she'll see what I've put up with all this time." This thinking may have been part of the reason I had a recurring nightmare that my pillow grew arms and tickled me to death. To this day, I do not lay down with my armpits exposed.

Because everything had feelings, it was a struggle to pass them by in the store, knowing they were just calling out to come home with me. "Don't leave me here!" I could hear them saying. "They treat me terribly! Ken touches me inappropriately at night! I'm afraid the stuffed elephant is a psychopath! Please, I need a good home!" My heart strings would be tugged, and the uglier the toy, the harder the pull. Only I could love that stuffed armadillo with one eye the way he deserved to be loved! I must have him and make him mine!

Having grown up with the parents I did, it is easy to understand why I am the way I am. My mom is more of a collector, nothing crazy, unless you consider her love of wrapping paper nuts. I'll admit to inheriting this, a quality that she herself inherited from her mother, who inherited it from her mother. Our Diet Coke addition seems to have also passed through these lines.

Mom is not afraid to buy things she needs, but my dad owned the same five white dress shirts for 30 plus years. The shirts were worn so thin they were nearly Emperor's New Clothes proportions. When my dad died, one of the hardest things to throw away was a sliver of soap he had been using. Never wanting to waste what he had, when a sliver of soap got too small to effectively use, he would attach it to a new bar of soap. In his honour, I didn't throw his soap sliver away, but added it to a new bar. I also seem to have inherited his distaste of wasting things, which, when applied inappropriately, can feed the hoarder in me.

When my parents decided to downsize to a new home, they began getting rid of things they had accumulated for years. While my mom was good at letting things go, my dad held on a bit tighter, seeing more value in things he thought he could sell. He didn't claim his items had feelings, but that they still had 'a lot of life' in them. In order to help him let go, I decided I would do him a favor and take a lot of his items off his hands. I pretended I wanted whatever item he was loath to take to the thrift store, he gave it to me happily, then, unbeknownst to him, I donated it. It is what I would want someone to do for me. Be the middleman in a game of decluttering. Those who watched me do this shook their heads at the unnecessary extra step, but I'm a good daughter, and I understood my dad's plight.

It wasn't until I was married and moved into my own apartment that I realized I had too much 'stuff'. Every time we moved, and we did that a lot, I would have to pack it all or find a way to get rid of it that didn't involve throwing it away. Like my dad, I couldn't bear to throw perfectly good things away. After all, I didn't want to hurt anything's feelings. How would I feel if my husband decided he didn't have room for me anymore, and just threw me away? (Oh wait, that totally happened.)

Much to the chagrin of my local thrift shop, they were forced to sift through the mounds of regretfully let go items; much of which they probably threw away. It isn't that I wanted them to have to throw away my shit, it is just that I couldn't bring myself to do it. If they did it, the bitterness of old tablecloths and socks would fall upon their heads, not mine.

After my second divorce to the same man-child, I found myself displaced from the 3,700-square foot beautiful brick palace we shared, resettling in a 1,000-square foot mobile home. While I loved my place, I realized I had too many things to reasonably fit inside and still have the place look liveable. I decided to embrace the idea of minimalism.

It can be said (and has been) that I have a bit of an obsessive personality. It is seen in my collecting, and in my all encumbering diets and lifestyle changes. Usually, I'll be obsessed with something for a few weeks or months, then move on to something new. I was this way with knitting, scrapbooking, and woodworking. I am absurdly good at being an easily distracted jack of all trades and an unfocused master of none.

I have always loved organizing things, and I realized that my organized things would look even more organized if I had less of them. Fancy that! I started getting rid of items with an almost feverish abandon. Within three weeks, I had easily gotten rid of over 3,000 items. The problem was, I was still obsessed with the idea of minimalism, and I didn't have anything else to get rid of. So, I did what any person raised in a religion based in converting would do; I tried to impose my minimalism on other people.

Starting with my kids, I would ask, "Do you want that? Do you need this?" My son, unattached to items, could have gotten rid of everything he owned without an eye. My daughter, on the other hand, seems to be more sentimental, and has a harder time letting go. Back and forth we would go, me, trying to get her to donate old toys, and her, reminding me of why she needed to keep them. Eventually, since most of their toys reside in the much larger home of their father, I gave up and decided their mess can be his problem.

For my fiancé, on the other hand, I am still his problem. He will often come home to changes in furniture, décor, and appliances. It's a good thing he isn't sight impaired, though he is with me, so you could debate his visual ability.

He puts up with my fervour of minimalism the same way he puts up with my diet overhauls and my impulsive decisions. With grace and good nature. Time will tell if he snaps one day, making me just another story on Forensic Files. For now, I will continue to suppress my hoarding tendencies by combating them with the power of minimalism. As for you, dear reader, just take comforting knowing you don't hoard jugs of pee and small animal carcasses. Unless you do, in which case, I'd be happy to come help you 'minimalize'.

Just Say No!

My entire life I have been groomed to not make a scene. My father comes from a long line of ancestors who believed wholeheartedly that children should be seen and not heard. This was incredibly hard for me, as I was prone to be loud and obnoxious wherever I went. I'm still this way.

After not seeing my dad for nearly two years, the first words he said to me were, "Why do you talk so loud?" Not, "It is great to see you," or, "I missed you so much." They were "Why do you talk so loud? Could you please talk softer?"

Being raised in a family of six kids, it is imperative to talk the loudest in order to be heard. The squeaky wheel gets the grease after all. Being loud worked well for me when I was in law enforcement, but not so much when I worked in a library.

I'm usually only loud when I am around people I'm comfortable with. If I'm with strangers or people I don't know that well, I'm generally very quiet, choosing to observe what is around me rather than speak. If someone I don't know asks me to do something, I will usually do it, no matter what it is. As a child, I learned the path of least resistance is also the path that creates no drama; and one that prevents me from getting a butt whoopin'. This is how I almost was kidnapped back in 1992. Dramatic, right?

My family often travelled, and this particular time we were in Kansas City Missouri, probably for some church thing. Growing up Mormon, almost everything you do is for 'some church thing'. It was one of my brother's birthdays, and most likely to apologize for doing boring church stuff on his birthday, my parents took us to the mall to look at toys.

While my brother looked around with the promise of a new and shiny something, the rest of us grumbled and shifted from foot to foot, complaining that 'it wasn't fair'. Instead of making myself miserable and eyeing toys I couldn't have, I decided to stand outside the toy store and glare in, hoping my parents would change their mind about buying me a toy.

I was standing there glaring when a tall, blond man, perhaps in his early twenties, wearing jeans and a ratty flannel shirt approached me.

"Hey, I really need your help," he said, looking a bit desperate.

My mind immediately started flashing big, red warning signs. This was a stranger. A strange man, nonetheless. I knew better than to talk to him, so of course I replied, "Okay."

"I need you to follow me for a minute." He looked around nervously.

"Okay," I repeated, attempting to calculate in my mind how much trouble I would get in for not staying in the store vs. creating a potential scene by telling this man no and running away. I decided I could always pretend I just went to the bathroom and return before my parents even noticed I was gone.

Mr Creeper and I began walking, making a few turns through the mall, when he pointed out another man across the hall.

"Alright, here is what I need help with. That man over there has been following me. I need you to go distract him for me."

I eyed the man across the hall, noting that he looked like he murdered little kids and ate them on his days off.

"What do I do?" I asked him, wondering what exactly he thought I was naive enough to do, despite the fact that I had already followed a strange man across the mall for no apparent reason other than rampant stupidity.

"I don't care," he said impatiently, "just go talk to him."

Rather than be forced to talk to Mr Creepy any longer, I nodded and headed cautiously towards the man he pointed at, who stood leaning against a wall looking menacing. I walked very slowly and watched out of the corner of my eye as Mr Creepy skulked away, looking suspicious as hell while trying to look nonchalant.

The moment he was far enough away, I took off running back towards the toy store, ignoring the enraged 'Hey come back here!' from the man across the hall. My suspicions were confirmed, they were working together.

I hauled ass, ignoring confused looks by other mall patrons, and skidded into the store, sliding up to my dad, knowing that this man, the one who would deliver a noteworthy ass spanking would also defend me from a kidnapper; even if I was dumb enough to have followed him.

"Go wait with your mom," my dad said, proving that he had not even known I was gone.

"Maybe I should have gotten kidnapped," I muttered to myself. "That would show him."

Luckily, my potential kidnappers did not follow me, though I kept an eye out for the rest of the day, sure that they would come get their revenge and snatch me up.

You'd think that such a harrowing experience would prevent me from making future bad decisions. But no. I would forever be giving people more information about myself than needed, just to spare feelings or not make a scene. I assumed that if I refused to give the freak at the bus stop my number, he would start yelling and flailing his arms, eventually pulling out a bazooka and blowing us all to Kingdom Come.

Or something like that.

When I was in college, I took the bus and the train everywhere I went. Anyone who takes public transportation knows that you meet some unsavoury characters while commuting together. More often than I would have liked, some strange man would strike up a conversation with me. Not wanting to be rude, I would politely respond. Usually things would end up fine, my only injury a few minutes of being uncomfortable. However, I'd also have days where I wished I had been meaner.

"Hey, I just wanted to tell you that you are so stunningly beautiful."

Across from me sat a man in his thirties, staring me up and down in a way that made the hairs on the back of my neck stand up.

"Oh!" I replied. "Thank you! That is nice of you to say." I turned slightly towards the window, praying he would leave it at that.

"Just speaking the truth," he continued. "I'd never lie to such a gorgeous woman."

Inwardly, I rolled my eyes, thinking he needed to slow his roll, because I was half his age. Also, I wasn't even that good looking. Outwardly, I smiled politely, and continued looking out the window. Suddenly, he was holding my hand.

I looked down at our hands, looked up at his face, then back down at his hand, fingers softly brushing my own. My brain could not compute how he could possibly find this appropriate, nor could it decipher a way to get out of this situation without creating a scene.

So what did I do? I froze. And I let him hold my damn hand!

For thirty minutes!

At this point in my life I had never kissed a boy, much less held anyone's hand. As uncomfortable as this douche was making me, I was also mad. How dare he take away my first handholding experience!

As I sat, willing a black hole to swallow me up, he continued talking about how beautiful I was, and asking me questions about where I went to school and where I lived. I gave vague answers, all the while being painfully polite. I asked where he was scheduled to get off, so I could get off somewhere, anywhere, else. Naturally, he was getting off at the same stop I was.

Rather than endure another moment of weirdness, the moment the train stopped I stood up, breaking our sweaty grip and feeling satisfaction at his dismayed face.

"This is my stop!" I exclaimed as I headed toward the door. "It was nice to meet you!"

I stepped off the train just as the doors were closing, preventing him from following me, all the while cursing myself for telling him it was nice to meet him. No, it was not nice to meet him. It was awful, and he was a creep, and now I had to wait 20 minutes for the next train to get to the stop I needed. I hated him, and I hoped he tried to hold hands with a piranha next time.

Most of the time I say nothing in situations like these. I let the moment play its course, accepting the collateral damage as just part of my womanly burden. Then, later, I stew about it, kicking myself for not being more of a feminist, and not valuing my own personal comfort over some fucking weirdo's desire to feel a connection.

I am attempting to teach my children the near opposite of what I was taught. Not all authority is going to have your best interest at heart. Just because they are older than you, does not mean you need to automatically do what they tell you without questioning it. If it feels wrong, run away, tell someone, or beat the living hell out of the aggressor if need be. Scenes be damned.

My goal for myself, as well as my children, is to be able to stand up to people who are attempting to take advantage. Instead of cowardly giving someone my phone number, I want to have the courage to say, "No, that isn't appropriate." I don't want to add 'I'm sorry' at the end, or even an apologetic smile. I just want to be able to say no.

As I'm writing this, I'm also sending an email to my daughter's school, agreeing to volunteer for something I really don't want to do. An activity requiring hours of work and no reward. Obviously, I have a lot of work to do in learning how to say no. But hey, at least no one is holding my hand.

Lazy Eye Laura

There may not be anything more profound in a person's life than a flaw they cannot do anything about. These flaws shape them into the person they become, good or bad. This happened to me with my crossed-eyes.

I wonder what my parents thought when I opened my eyes for the first time as a baby. I'm guessing they assumed it would pass, and my eyes would end up facing the right direction. Most new-borns are cross-eyed now and then. I imagine they waited, and waited, and waited, only to discover my eyes were stuck that way. Perhaps in the womb I had been making faces, and no one bothered to tell me my face would get stuck that way. Whatever the reason, it did, and it not only shaped the direction of my eyes, but also my life.

I had two eye surgeries when I was a child, around age two, in which the doctors went into my eye sockets and hacked away like an angry arborist. I'm sure they surgeons did the best they could back in the 1980s, but it is possible that they went to a medical school taught by Edward Scissorhands himself. Whatever the result, it wasn't perfectly aligned eyes. I again had two surgeries in my 20s, with similar results. After my fourth surgery, I was told that my left eye was now perfectly in place, but that my right eye compensated, and started crossing because it was unused to the alignment. Figures, right?

I don't remember the first time someone made fun of my eyes, though I imagine it was while I was pretty young. Kids are shitty that way. But kids are also great because they don't realize they should be offended by comments or questions. I remember being that way as a child. When someone would ask me why my eyes were weird, I would tell them I was born with a lazy eye, no shame whatsoever.

I never did like the term lazy-eye. It sounded as if my eye determined it would rather sit in a lawn chair and drink margaritas instead of doing its damn job. Not that I would blame it, but as a body part, you kind of have to do what is needed. The punishment is often being removed, which seems a terrible waste. I imagine appendices everywhere screaming as they are cut out, "I'm just kidding! I'll start doing my job! I just got so lazy I forgot what I actually do! Just don't kill me, please! I'll be good!"

It must have been around first grade when I began being hurt by people's remarks. I had just moved with my family to a new town, and I was not wanting to 'stand out' in the slightest. The problem was, I had a very specific fashion sense.

I had a habit of wearing brightly coloured clothes, creating outlandish combinations of accessories and clothing. I made a statement with what I wore, and most often, that statement was, "I'm weird! Make fun of me mercilessly!"

It was around that time that I also begged my parents to stop making me wear a sticky eye patch over my right eye. The point of the eye patch was to force that lazy bastard of a left eye to get with the program. But it was hot and sweaty under that eye patch, and I would get asked constantly why I had a band aid over my eye. With my verbal prowess, I convinced them to let me start wearing a pirate eye patch.

Oh, how I loved that eye patch. I still have it to this day! It was made of soft black material, and dark green on the inside. It had a stretchy bit that went over my head and held it in place nicely. When I put it on, I felt tough, invincible, and like a badass pirate. At least, until I realized other people didn't find it nearly as cool.

I have often lamented our loss of innocence. We are born with strong personalities, which somehow fade with social pressure. We are forced to fit in with the rest of society. While that may be a good thing for potential serial killers and rapists, it is hard on those who have malformed bodies, differing sexual identities, or are just plain quirky. I miss the days where I didn't care what people thought of how I looked or dressed. I knew I was great, no matter what. I lost that somewhere early on, and it makes me sad.

Despite other kids' opinions on my pirate patch, I still wore it, if only because my parents said I had to. I began to hate it, because it was difficult to read, as my left I would smoosh letters together, and I was unable to determine what words said. When I took off the patch, I could read everything perfectly, because my right eye would take over. This would eventually cause a million issues on driving tests and eye tests of all kinds. Yes, I can see fine. No, I can't tell what letters are there. Yes, I promise I'm not blind.

I don't think I wore the eye patch more than a few months before my constant bitching at my parents about how it annoyed me got the best of them. They let me retire it to my memory box, and I went along my life without it.

The problem of no eye patch was that it became incredibly obvious how my eyes did not match up. I couldn't hide behind a patch anymore. I was forced to be honest with my gaze. When I would look at someone in class, they would look behind them to see who I was talking to. When I would visit my grandparents, I would get lectures on looking folks in the eye when you spoke to them. You look dishonest if you don't. I realized I would always look dishonest, because I would be looking someone in the eye, but they would think I wasn't. I couldn't win, could I?

Over the years of being made fun of for my eyes, I became a more compassionate person. If I saw someone with a disability or disfigurement, I understood a bit more of what they were going through. I could tell when they were ashamed, sad, or lonely. I saw the frustration in their faces when having to describe what exactly was 'wrong'. I became someone who would do almost anything to make someone else feel comfortable.

I became a better person, though I'm still annoyingly sensitive about my eyes. When people bring up my eyes I still cringe inside. I still feel that hot embarrassment whenever someone looks behind them to see who I am talking to. But I am stronger, funnier, and more resilient to ridicule than I would have been without my flaw.

They say God doesn't make mistakes, which we all know is a lie. But if there is a God, He/She certainly does have a sense of humour about the mistakes made. I'm just grateful I could be in on the joke. The butt of it certainly, but in on it nonetheless.

My Mission

Growing up Mormon is um, incredibly interesting, to say the least. Like many religions, it involves all sorts of religious dogma that shape the ideas and foundations of its members. Mormons place a huge emphasis on serving a proselyting mission for the church. Traditionally, this is mostly geared at the boys. While the boys are being groomed to go serve in foreign lands for two years, the girls are being groomed to get married and have children. Yes, I think this is completely whack, and I am grateful this seems to be changing, even minutely.

I always wanted to go on a mission. It wasn't that I wanted to teach people about Jesus Christ (which I certainly don't have a problem with, and is the whole point of going on a mission), it was just that I wanted to help people and show my love to others. I have always been compassionate, wanting to help those less fortunate than myself.

Mormons are 'called' to serve missions, and do not get to choose where they go. They are assigned to an area of the world by one of the church's 12 apostles. These apostles don't know much, if anything, about the people they are assigning. Mormons believe that God, working through his disciples, is sending the missionaries to the place that they are meant to be. I, apparently, was meant to be in Sydney, Australia.

I left my family in February of 2004, entering the Missionary Training Centre (MTC) for two weeks to begin an intense training program on how to teach people about the gospel of Jesus Christ. We had to study scriptures for hours on end, and host 'practice' discussions with volunteer members of the church posing as investigators. They would ask questions that we would stumble through answering, never sure what we were doing or what the 'correct' answer was.

Missionaries are given the title of Elder or Sister. You are referred to as 'Elder' if you are a male, or 'Sister' if you are female. I was Sister Roper, and I wasn't sure how I felt about it.

As a Sister Missionary, you were required (at least at the time I served) to dress as much like an old crone as possible. If anyone could look at you with anything other than mild irritation and intrigue, you were dressed inappropriately. Mormons are a modest people in general, but as missionaries, you are not to show any skin other than lower arms, face, and neck. And you definitely shouldn't have a personality full of quirks like mine.

While in the MTC, as with the rest of your mission, you are assigned to another missionary, and you as a pair are considered 'companions'. You are required to do everything with your companion, except, you know, bathroom stuff. Everywhere you walk, you walk together. You sleep in the same room, eat with each other, and smell each other's farts. You are meant to hold one another accountable for one another's actions, thereby keeping you both righteous and rule-obeying.

My MTC companion was a convert to the church; meaning only that she was not born within it but joined later on in life. She was a sweet girl, from Michigan, and was much more into the idea of being 'good' at everything than I was. She was a health nut, and thanks to her judgmental 'tsks', I found myself pretending to not want to eat all the candy and birthday cake my mom sent me via mail. In reality, I would hide it and eat it in a bathroom stall during my only moments of privacy, looking like Gollum with his precious. I'd exit the bathroom, breath sweet and blood sugar surging, only to have to go with her to the gym for 'exercise time'.

She was always disappointed that I didn't want to run laps with her. But why would I? I was a chunky, out of shape motherfucker who just wanted to eat candy in peace. So, while she would be jogging around the track, I would set up shop on an exercise mat, occasionally doing a sit up, but really napping.

Sleep was a thing of the past in the MTC. I had grown accustomed to taking a nap every now and then, not the strict 10:45 p.m. bed time and 6:00 a.m. wake up. It didn't help that the food, although very tasty, was heavy and made me sleepy for the hours upon hours that I had to sit in class. Between the food and the lack of sleep, I was eager to leave the MTC.

Thankfully, my time at the MTC only lasted two weeks, then I was off to Australia to meet my new companion, and deal with serious jet lag for the next few weeks.

I loved Australia, and even though Australians had absolutely no interest in hearing about Mormonism, they were polite enough, and taught me more than I could ever have taught them. I had several companions from all around the world, who taught me about humility and kindness, as well as how to get along with others. I learned how to ride a bike up steep heels while wearing a dress, and to fall off a bike, going down steep hills, after getting said dress tangled in the spokes of the wheels.

I got to see my first ever naked man on my mission, as many men found it funny to see our faces turn red when they answered the door in the nude. I may have been unimpressed with the men when they were nude, but I was very impressed when they were clothed. In Australia, the men's shorts seem to be inexplicably shorter than the women's, like the stores got confused and set the women's shorts in the men's section. This is a style I can get behind. If only because I'd rather wear shorts that cover my cellulite, while gawking and giggling at men's hairy upper thighs.

When arriving in Australia I expected all men to look like Thor. I was worried I wouldn't be able to keep my mind on God when an Asgard sent fertility god was eyeing me across the way. The media and hunks like the Hemsworth brothers fed into my notions of gorgeous Australian men.

God's work must have had fortune on its side, because I never did find a Thor of my own; or anyone even remotely resembling a god. I did, however, come across multiple men with no teeth and 'crotch rocket' swimmers. Australian men sure do love speedos. I suppose if you wrestle crocodiles and dodge gigantic spiders all day you aren't worried about looking manly. Or maybe, speedos are the ultimate manly attire. As manly as I myself may be, I really wouldn't know.

I learned fun new phrases like 'kick a tin around' and 'get bent, ya dodgy cunt'. I learned how to take rejection with good grace, and to get around Australia while driving on the other side of the road. As it turns out, I still drive on the 'other side of the road' when I'm unduly tired or late at night (Don't tell the DMV).

Serving as a missionary, you meet all types of people, and often learn lessons from them you never could have imagined. I learned that you could fall off a 90-foot cliff and survive with only a broken nose, earn the name the 'Miracle Man', and go on to live your life having been famous in the land down under for a short time. It didn't matter that he fell off a cliff while dangling over it for comedic effect, or that he wandered around the bottom of the cliff for hours, half naked, suffering from hypothermia. What would have been a miracle would have been a group of 19-year-old boys not acting the fool and hanging off cliffs. But hey, anything for a good conversion starter! After the story of his fall hit the news, we were encouraged to use it as an icebreaker. "Hey, would you like to hear more about The Church of Jesus Christ of Latter-Day Saints? No? Alright. How about the 'Miracle man'? He's a Mormon, you know. That's right. He's one of us! Survived by God's grace!"

No matter the ploy we used, the opening liner or the go to story, Australians just don't seem to be all that excited about religion. To be honest, even though it was my job to hype them up for my religion, I admired them when they told me, "I can't be bothered to care about religion." Talk about honesty! How refreshing! No wonder they are such a peaceful people! They don't get their knickers in a twist over something as trite as the afterlife and possible eternal damnation. This may be the greatest lesson I learned from Australians. They are the very definition of 'chill'.

After serving 18 months of 24-hour service to God and man, I flew home, waving goodbye to the land down under and its short man shorts. Taking off at the airport, I heaved a sigh of relief that God's work would go on without me, because I was exhausted. Mormon missions are no joke. They are hard work combined with constant rejection. I sat back in my seat for the 18-hour flight to L.A. and imagined the loving reunion my family would have waiting for me back in Utah.

Mormons are notorious for having over the top welcoming committees for their precious servants of the Lord. If you have ever been to the Salt Lake City International Airport, you've seen large groups of people gathered with signs, balloons, and flowers, welcoming 'Elder Jones' or 'Sister Young' back from their service. Personally, I've always found it obnoxious. Until it was my turn to be the centre of that adoring attention.

I rushed from the plane and down the hall, excited to see my family once again after all that time away. Since missionaries are only allowed to call home twice a year on Mother's Day and Christmas, I had not spoken to them in months.

I got to the top of the escalator, ready to descend, and saw the groups gathered at the bottom. My eyes wandered over the many clusters of people, looking for mine. Only, there wasn't a group of people for me. There were no welcoming signs, no balloons, nothing. While all around me other missionaries hugged their families, I stood twiddling my thumbs in the corner. Occasionally another group would throw a pitying glance my way, but for the most part I was unobserved, all alone, immersed in self-pity.

Finally, after what seemed like an eternity, I saw my dad's head above the crowd. I snuck up behind him and said, "You looking for me?" He turned, returned the hug I forced upon him, and remarked that it was nice to see me. After a few more minutes the rest of my family arrived, full of apologies and hugs. Because I was still a good Christian, I forgave them their trespasses, and just enjoyed the moment. For that short time, I was the star. People wanted me, and not one of them told me to 'go eat a dirty wanker'. All in all, a good reunion.

The next time you see those naïve young missionaries with their conservative clothing and black name tags, remember to treat them with compassion, and, for the love of God, answer the door fully clothed.

Mouse House and Rat Maze

Someone (I think and hope a cat), left a severed mouse head on my doormat the other morning. I opened the door, saw a small grey head with a red and bloodied stump, and I did what any woman in my situation would do. I blamed my fiancé.

"Ewwwww!" I yelled at him while he stood shaving in the bathroom. "There is a mouse head on the doormat! Did you drop it there?"

Before I continue, let me say that it was a fair assumption. You see, the previous evening, in the middle of the night, he returned home from work with a half-dead rat. Why would he do such a thing? Let me enlighten you.

My fiancé is what some would call a bug nerd. Along with unknown amounts of ant colonies, he owns two giant centipedes. They are hideous and creepy, and I hate them. But they make him happy, and he makes me happy, so I allow them in my house. So, when he came home with a half-dead rat to feed to his centipedes, I wasn't as upset about that as I was knowing I had just let go of some foul-smelling gas, thinking he wouldn't be home for another seven hours. When he entered the bedroom to say hi, I hadn't had time to cover the smell.

"Hey, boo," he said, pausing before he continued. "What's that smell?"

I panicked, knowing that he would immediately dump me if I admitted to creating that stench.

"Popcorn," I supplied, choosing the first thing to pop in my mind that might remotely resemble the smell.

"You sure?" He took a deep breath in through his nose and I cringed. "It smells like rotten eggs."

"Really?" I tried to sound confused. "I can't really smell anything with this cold."

Thankfully, he dropped it and left to go kill a small creature for the benefit of an even smaller one. Before he headed back to work, he shouted, "Love you boo! I'll be back to clean up the body tomorrow!" I wasn't even phased by that sentence. Thus is my life.

Therefore, when I saw the mouse head, I assumed he had dropped it on his way to the trash can. After further inspection, we discovered that it was the head of a completely separate rodent. We were starting to collect enough mouse parts to create our own little house of horrors.

My fiancé was flattered with the gift left by our cat, while I was a little disconcerted. Occasionally I will have flashbacks to traumatic events in my past, and the mouse head spurred a particularly disturbing one of the neighbours who lived down the road.

Melissa Shorneck (whom I always thought of as Missy Shortneck) was awful. She was a blond-haired bully of epic proportions. I should have been suspicious when she asked if I wanted to see her new toy, but I was dumb and trusting and just grateful to have someone to talk to. I agreed, and she led me down into her basement.

Down we went, into a dark corner. Looking around for brightly coloured and girly toys, I was confused.

"Where is it?" I asked, still searching in the dark.

"Right there. In the corner. See that?"

I looked harder and saw a lump of dark grey fur.

"What is it?"

She looked at me like I was an idiot, which I was.

"It's a fake rat. Really realistic. I like to scare my family with it. Go on, touch it. It feels real."

I crept closer and held out a finger. I poked it and giggled.

"Ewww, it does feel real! I bet that freaks people out!" I poked it again.

"You can borrow it if you want. I've got another one. Actually, you can have it. I already scared everyone I know with it." She shrugged off her gift as if it was nothing, but I was delighted.

"No way! Thank you! Ha ha. I can't wait to scare my mom." I picked it up and squeezed it, half hoping it would have eyes that popped out when I did. Instead, it was a confusing mix of stiff and squishy. I put it in my shirt pocket, and felt like the character from my favorite book, *The Indian in the Cupboard*. (I'm not sure if that book was racist, but as a kid I was crazy about the idea of owning my own little friend).

I named the rat Reginald and off we went. I spent the day outside riding my bike, playing on our neighbourhood's 'dirt hill' (which was, in fact, a dirt hill) and talking to Reginald the entire time.

"Look, Reginald," I would say with gusto, "that's a corn field! And over there is a big tree!" (There weren't a lot of interesting things to see in our town).

After hours of playing, we finally went home to scare mom. Reginald laid down on the floor in the kitchen, and I hid around the corner and watched. And watched, and watched. Finally, my mom came in, took one look at the mouse on the floor, got a large spoon from the cupboard, and scooped it up, headed for the trash.

"No!" I yelled, coming out of my corner. "Don't throw it away! It is fake! See?" I grabbed Reginald off the spoon and began waving it in my mom's face.

"Look! Look how real it is! Feel it!" I squeezed it near mom's face and watched her lean back in disgust.

"That's not a fake mouse, Laura." I stared at her.

"Yes, it is! Melissa gave it to me. She said it is a fake rat and it is supposed to scare people."

My mom shook her head and pointed towards the trash.

"Now I know it isn't fake. How long have you been carrying this around? Throw it away."

I stood, and, for the first time, really looked at Reginald. Instead of Halloween-isque fun, I saw a corpse in the beginning stages of rigor mortis. Rather than little marble eyes, I saw clouded over balls of tissue. And yet, part of me still wanted to keep it. We had bonded, that little dead rat and I. Sadly, I put Reginald in the trash, sniffing my fingers as a final goodbye.

"That's disgusting," my mom said as she took the trash outside to the garage. "Go wash your hands before you get the plague."

I'm not sure why I didn't clue in to the prank pulled by that damn Missy Shortneck. I suppose I had hoped she was going to be my friend. I was always thinking idiotic things like that. I should have at the very least smelled the rot; I was used to that smell.

Sometimes at parties, just for an icebreaker, I mention that the first corpse I ever smelled was coming from my bedroom wall growing up. This is not a lie, though to the disappointment of my audience, the body belonged to a dead mouse, not the friendly neighbourhood hobo.

Iowa is covered in fields, a great breeding ground for mice. There are lots of mice roaming around, looking for good places to build nests. Every year, a few of them would find their way into our walls, and I would fall asleep listening to the pitter patter of mice running up and down the planks, imagining monsters scratching, attempting to get out of the walls, not furry little friends building homes inside them.

Occasionally, the mice must have lost a loved one due to old age, spider bite, or that plague my mom had warned me about. They would hold a little funeral for their friend, then leave the corpse to rot where it was, usually in a spot near my bed. Thankfully, this is the only time (thus far) I have smelled a body decaying.

While I could appreciate the mice wanting to build a home within my home, my favorite mouse house was at a seasonal fair called 'Cornbelly's'. Around Halloween time, the doors to the fair open, and kids and adults head out for pumpkin picking, spooky scare houses, and hayrides.

The only year I went, I brought my five-year-old daughter and six-year-old son. We had enjoyed the hayride and picked our pumpkins when we came across a large wooden box with clear sides. Within the box, there was a maze, just big enough for little kids to crawl through from beginning to end. At the entrance, in large random fonts, read 'The Rat Maze'.

While the Rat Maze is a thing of claustrophobic nightmares to me now, as a child I would have loved it. Kids are dumb, not knowing the dangers of crawling through a large box with only one exit, the plastic siding serving as a magnifying glass, the sun attempting to roast children like ants.

"Look!" I exclaimed using the voice I only bring out to encourage my kids to do something they wouldn't ordinarily do on their own. "Doesn't that look fun?"

My daughter readily agreed and got in line behind the other children eager to go in. My son, after some convincing, eventually joined his sister. I stood back and watched as they climbed in, then moved to the side to get a better look.

Upon closer inspection, I saw the utter madness that was happening inside. Children were piled on each other, too packed in to turn back, but unable to find the exit. One after another, they began panicking, unable to move, squashed like chickens in inhumane farms. They began to scream and cry, terrified of never seeing freedom again.

Parents on the side tried to single out their children, yelling directions to them.

"Go to your left, Byron! No, your left! Remember, you make an L with your thumb and finger to find left."

"Sarah, you need to back up just a little bit…look out for the kid behind you…you need to turn around! It's okay, you're fine!"

Parent after parent began losing their cool, fearing for the safety and well-being of their beloved children. A few sensitive souls even began to cry. I looked into the maze, saw my bawling children, and I began to laugh. Uncontrollable, tears streaming, laughter. Seeing the fear in their eyes made my shoulders shake and my breath come in short bursts.

People around me shot me the dirtiest looks I've ever gotten, a few even asking me what kind of person would laugh at a time like that. And I realized, I would. I, Laura, would laugh in the face of fear. Other people's fear, that is. Children's fear. Children who were stuck in a giant wooden box called The Rat Maze. Children who, if they ever got out, would probably suffer from PTSD. Imagining their future therapy sessions, I laughed harder, feeling like I might vomit.

"I just don't know, doctor," the grown child might say. "I just have this irrational feeling I'm going to be stuck somewhere. Like a box. Or a maze."

"What's so funny?" My mother-in-law asked coming up behind me. Mid wheeze, I pointed behind me at the mayhem.

"You are a terrible person," she said before attempting to comfort my kids.

I don't know how, when, or why they were able to escape The Rat Maze, but I do know that it is one of my favorite memories. I laugh every single time I think about it. To me, life is just one, giant rat maze. There is screaming, crying and the feeling of being trapped. Unlike the Rat Maze, we won't make it out alive. We will, I imagine, look out in terror, and see the face of someone laughing uncontrollably. Isn't it great?

Proud Parenting

I always imagined my kids would get in trouble with the law at some point in their lives; after all, the apple never falls far from the tree, right? I just didn't expect to have a visit from a Sheriff's deputy before my kids had even reached age seven!

In retrospect, I don't know why I was surprised. My father, who was a very law-abiding citizen in adulthood, was a very 'naughty' kid. He, when feeling cheeky, would recount stories of running from the cops and hiding in nearby sewer pipes to avoid detection. Usually he was guilty of the kind of 'boys will be boys' behaviour that would get him arrested today. Douchey boy-things like throwing snowballs at cars or setting off firecrackers under school room doors. While I certainly don't condone this behaviour, it made for a good story, and made my straight-laced father seem more human.

Dad was able to get all that bad behaviour out of his system and move on to lead a productive and honest life. I, however, never seemed to grow out of that 'naughty' phase, and routinely struggle with the minor rules of society. (Chill out, I said 'minor' rules.)

So, when I opened the door and saw the Sherriff's deputy standing there, I had to wonder who he was there for. I mentally tallied all my wrong doings and determined he couldn't possibly be there for me. I breathed a sigh of relief which lasted all of five seconds.

"Ma'am, we've had a complaint."

My mind went wild again. Was it the damn neighbour across the street who yelled at me for my dog's occasional barks and romps through the neighbourhood? Perhaps the complaint was not so much the dog's running free but the owner's screaming of obscenities while she chased the damn dog down the street.

Did I walk across the house again in my underwear with the blinds open? Sure, I could see how people could find that disturbing, but it is also quite fascinating. How does one jiggle in so many places all at once? Really, kids should do a science fair project on me. Am I solid? Am I liquid? No one really knows! Why turn me into the cops?

Most likely the neighbours overheard me yelling at my kids, who seemed to have taken after their mother in terms of behaviour. Possibly, they heard me threatening to tie them to a tree and let the birds peck at them. Truthfully though, I couldn't be sure. The possibilities of why the law was at my door were endless.

"Okay…" I hedged. "About what?"

He shuffled from foot to foot, looking a little nervous.

"Do you have kids, ma'am?"

Oh shit! It was about the kids. Think, Laura, think! What did you do in public, with witnesses? My mind went blank. I couldn't come up with anything I'd done wrong. I took a millisecond to feel proud.

"Yes, I have a four-year-old daughter and a six-year-old son. He's autistic." I always throw that last bit in there in case it will help our cause. So sue me.

"Can I see the shoes they were wearing this morning?" The plot immeasurably thickened. Where on earth was this going?

"They are wearing them right now, and they are at a birthday party. What exactly is going on?" I stared at him, looking for clues.

"Well," he started, "a neighbour stated that your kids were climbing on her car, leaving significant damage to the vehicle."

I cringed, but I wasn't ultimately worried. I knew the cars in my neighbourhood, and a good description of most of them would be 'junkyard rejects'. However, in keeping with the tradition of parents everywhere, I became instantaneously defensive.

"When did this supposedly happen? They were here with me today. And whose car is it? Why didn't they just call me if they saw this?" It was Detective Laura on the case, turning the deputy into the one being questioned. He took my passive-aggressive attack well.

"I don't have an exact time, just that it happened this morning. The woman was visiting from California, so she didn't know whose kids they were. And, well, the car is a really nice corvette." He looked at me with unbridled adoration in his eyes, like her car was a national treasure. I looked at him dumbly. The last corvette I saw was my hot pink Barbie car I had at age eight. But if Barbie had it, it was probably an expensive car. I nervously scratched my arm, then berated myself for giving an outward sign of guilt.

He had the grace to look chagrined, seemingly waiting for me to explode with, "Don't you have anything better to do than harass little kids?" I knew he was just doing his job, so I cut him some slack.

"Well, I guess I can get the shoes when they get back from the party. I'll certainly talk to them." He seemed appeased at my assurance, said his farewell, and told me he'd be back later to collect the footwear.

The moment he left; I began scheming. What shoes did I have of the kids that were too big or too small? There must be prints on the car, and I couldn't just use a different shoe of the same size. That would be too transparent. If I didn't have any, could I borrow some? Perhaps I could frame some innocent neighbour kids? The kids up the street really got on my nerves.

Obviously, I needed to cover this up. It never even crossed my mind that my kids could be innocent. I knew better. They came by a life of crime naturally.

An hour later, my kids returned from the party and my interrogation began.

"Did the two of you climb on a red, shiny car this morning?" I looked them right in the eye, ready to play good mom bad mom.

"No." My daughter was quick with her lie, and I was proud. That's my kid! *She's a natural*, I thought, *she'll be ready to deny, deny, deny*. My son, bless his honest little soul, said, "Yes, we did, remember?" Damn it boy! I'd have to work with him.

"Okay," I said in my calm voice. "Why'd you do that?"

They both shrugged.

"Kaitlyn said we could," my son finally offered. "It's her grandma's car."

Bingo! I had found my angle of defence.

"Did Kaitlyn play on the car too?" I asked, praying she did.

"Yes, she told us we could, too." I mentally fist pumped the air. Score!

While my son spilled the details, my daughter remained silent. I decided to press her a bit. Looking at her, I lowered my voice.

"You didn't play on Kaitlyn's grandma's car?"

"No." She looked me right in the eye, not even blinking. My pride surged. I love a criminal who sticks to her story. I push further.

"Really? The police officer says your footprints are on the car."

"Not me," she tossed back, daring me to argue.

"Okay," I said. "Make sure you tell the policeman that when he comes back later today."

Fear crossed my son's face, while my daughter's remained impassive.

"Are we going to jail?" my son asked, concern mounting.

It was at this moment I realized I had a couple options. I could play the scared straight card, putting the fear of being taken to jail in handcuffs, and getting shanked in dark cold room into their little impressionable minds, or I could assure them they were going to be fine and that I'd take care of it. Even I was surprised when I answered,

"No, you aren't going to jail. But you should never touch someone else's property without their permission. Do you understand?" My son nodded solemnly.

"I didn't," my daughter maintained. *Good grief*, I thought, *I love this little liar.*

Later that day, the officer did come back for the shoes. Against my devious nature, I handed over the incriminating shoes they wore that morning. He came back not long after, bearing copies of the 'evidence'—shoeprints lifted off the corvette. I resisted rolling my eyes. He confirmed what I already knew. My children were in fact the culprits.

"I talked to them," I began. "They told me Kaitlyn also climbed on the car, and said it was okay. I did give them a lecture, but you can talk to them too if you like."

He entered the living room where the kids were waiting.

"I know you guys are still little," he said trying to successfully merge stern but not scary, "but you really caused a lot of damage to that lady's car."

"Not me," my daughter interrupted. I smiled to myself. Damn she's good. How is it possible to be a cherub and a devil simultaneously? Thankfully, the officer ignored her.

"You need to respect people's property, okay?" He shifted from foot to foot, obviously eager to get the hell out of the situation.

"Okay," the kids chorused, not meaning it, I was sure.

"Alright, then," the officer concluded, already heading toward the door. We said our awkward goodbyes at the door, and brushed my hands off, bemused that my kids had run ins with the law so much earlier than even I had.

I went back into the living room and stared at my little demon spawns.

"Well," I said. "Did you learn a lesson today?"

"Yes!" My son looked at me with big serious eyes. What a good boy. I turned to my daughter.

"Not me," she said.

Puberty is Gross

One of the saddest things you'll come across in parenting is the loss of your children's innocence. One minute they are chubby cheeked little cherubs, and the next they are long limbed pre-teens fiddling with their pocket-sized chubbies.

The first time I realized my baby boy was entering a more obnoxious and more disturbing phase of life was when I caught him watching a sex scene on Netflix. He was seven, ya'll, and my heart broke into a million pieces.

Truthfully, it is partially my fault. I was ignorant off all of the disturbing things that a young curious mind could view on Netflix when typing in 'sex'. I have since learned, obviously, of parental controls. I was unaware of them up until that point. No one has ever accused me of being the most technically savvy person out there.

The only reason I even discovered his foray into the darkness was his suspicious behaviour when I tried to enter the room. He met me in the hallway and immediately tried to push me away from the room. Red flags much? I might not have been all that Netflix smart, but he had a lesson or two to learn in the art of being sneaky. Everyone knows you have to act nonchalant, not guilty.

So, the moment he said, "Go away, Mom!" was the moment I knew he was in for it. Taking a page out of my own rulebook, I played it cool. I backed off, smiling to myself that he thought he had the upper-hand.

I went down the stairs, out the back door, and around the side of the house. It was easy, really. All I had to do was look up. Through the blinds, I saw as plain as day a pair of breasts, being fondled by disembodied hands.

"Ah, hell no!" I yelled out loud to myself. It was time for action.

Being the enlightened woman I am, I realized it was make or break time, and I had to make the right decision for both my current son and my future son. What I said and did now could scar him or leave him with an unhealthy view on sex. God forbid I be the cause of that. Instead of immediately losing my shit, I sat down on the driveway to ponder my next move. That is, after I flipped the power breaker to that entire section of the house. Watching the fondled breasts turn dark made me happier than I could have imagined.

Sitting and thinking about what to do, I remembered growing up in a very strict and religious home, where things like sex and nudity were never discussed, but we learned that they were 'bad' at church. When I was ten years old, I had to sit my mom down and ask her to explain menstruation to me. I also remember lifting my shirt and showing her 'cancer marks' on my stomach and thighs, only to be told they weren't cancer, but stretchmarks. So, it just goes to show you how much maturation education I had.

I mean, in fifth grade they show you a video that makes no sense at all. It shows some sort of cartoon ram's head, and little ball type things falling out of it every month. It was all a gobbledygook to me, and while the pad they handed out to us all made me feel somewhat sophisticated, I still didn't want anyone to know I had it. Even back then, I read the social queues that reminded me that a woman's natural bodily functions are disgusting and shameful.

Funnily enough, at the time I would have done anything to get my period. I remember asking all my older cousins when they got it, and if it really got rid of your baby fat. I begged them to tell me how to make it come faster, so that I could be a woman. Oh, how naïve I was! I had no idea what was in store!

I tried to encourage puberty to get started by convincing my cousin Jerica to teach me to shave my legs. What ended up happening looked like the scene from the film *Psycho*, after the character is murdered in the shower. From the waist down I was covered in nicks and cuts, and my aunt's bathtub was streaked with red.

My Edward Scissorhands attempt at shaving didn't encourage my period to arrive, so I had to settle for reading Judy Blum books and hoping for the best. Even though it felt like forever, my journey into womanhood came quickly, at the tender age of eleven. It took me approximately 2.5 seconds to realize I hated it, and womanhood can go to hell.

Menstruation is painful. At least it was for me. It also left me nauseous and with terrible cramps and diarrhoea. And not only did I hold on to my baby fat, I added to it significantly because the only thing that seemed to ease my discomfort was chocolate, French fries and ice cream.

In a nutshell, puberty blows. Years later, as I sat there on my driveway, reminiscing and wondering if puberty started earlier for kids now, I thought of ways to help my son navigate the nightmare that was about to take place in his body. Then I wondered if I would need therapy for being forced to think about my son's body and his maturation. Gross.

After a few more minutes, I returned to the house, went up the stairs, and found my son in his room.

"There's something wrong with the TV," he told me, looking more than a little disappointed.

"No," I said. "I turned it off."

He looked at me with indignation. "Why?"

This is the part I wanted to let loose on him. I wanted to say all the ignorant, ridiculous things that came to my mind. I wanted to tell him that he was just a baby, and that all those girls on TV have cooties of the worst variety. I wanted to guilt him into becoming a child again.

But I couldn't. I knew that if I did those things, I risked my son ever talking to me again about things that could make an impact. I also knew that his autism would make things more difficult for him, and that if he relied on TV for his knowledge, we would all be in trouble.

"I turned it off because…" I paused here, feeling my face begin to flame red, "that show really isn't for young kids to watch."

He stared me down, and I watched as realisation crossed his face. He immediately hid under a blanket. (To hide his shame, I assumed.)

"Hey, it's okay," I assured him, attempting to believe what I was saying. "You shouldn't be embarrassed that you like to see those things. Everyone does. People are curious about bodies and what they do. It is nothing to be ashamed of. You just have to know the right way to go about it."

I mentally patted myself on the back. I was crushing this parenting thing. No doubt about it. My son was going to be the most enlightened seven-year-old in the entire fucking world.

Eventually, he pulled the blanket off his head and looked at me. I patted him on the leg and tried to look like I had these talks every day.

"The important thing is to remember that not everything you see on TV is accurate. Things on TV aren't always real. And sometimes, what they show isn't what people are really like. Do you know what I mean?" He nodded, but I knew he had no idea.

"Do you have any questions about bodies, or anything like that?"

He dove right into it, typical autism style. "What is sex?" I inwardly cringed, but outwardly began a mini sex ed lesson talking about vaginas and penises, using the correct terms and feeling pretty good about my execution.

"Oh," he said after I finished. "Sometimes I have sex dreams."

This is the part I freaked the fuck out and lit the house on fire.

Okay, I didn't, but I wanted to. He was seven years old! Is that normal? Was he being molested? Why is he having dreams like that! Ewww! Ewww! Ewww!

"That is totally normal. It happens to everyone," is what I said.

"Does it happen to you?"

Ewwwww! Ewww! Ewww!

"Yes," I replied. "It is very normal. It is all part of growing up."

"Sometimes," he continued, "when I wake up, I have stuff in my underwear."

Holy shit! I was so not okay with my son having wet dreams. Especially when he should be dreaming of dinosaurs and baseball. Or whatever the hell little boys dream about. But shit. Apparently, they dreamed about sex. And I hated finding that out almost as much as I hated talking about it.

"Okay," I said attempting to control my blush, "that is called semen. It comes out of penises when they are excited." While remaining calm on the outside, on the inside I was screaming, *Sweet Jesus, please save me from this!*

"Okay," he said.

We stared at each other awkwardly until he said he was tired. Jesus came through!

"Well, you just let me know if you have any more questions, okay? I want to make sure you learn what is true. Not what the TV says is true. Okay?"

He nodded, and, with a goodnight kiss that somehow seemed less sweetly innocent than the night before, I left him to (hopefully) dream of dinosaurs and baseball.

A few days passed, and I had come to terms that my baby was growing up. I still mourned the loss of what he used to be, but I realized it was all going to be okay in the end.

One evening, about a month after our initial conversation, I took the kids to a carnival at their school. I stood chatting with several other moms while my son continually pulled on the leg of my pants. After many attempts at ignoring him, I finally snapped.

"What? I'm trying to have a conversation!"

"Mom, remember when you said that a girl's private part is called a vagina? I heard someone call it a pussy. Is that bad?"

All of the moms stared in horror at me, then began to slowly back away. It would seem that he chose that moment to take me up on my offer of enlightenment. I heaved a sigh and pulled him to the corner of the room.

"Well, you see…"

A fifteen-minute conversation took place in the school, huddled in a corner, on what terms are appropriate, and which can be offensive.

Fuck you, puberty. Stop haunting me already.

Sharkeisha, No!

I've always assumed I'd be killed by my cat eventually. I just figured it would be by tripping over it, hitting my head on a hard surface, and bleeding out. Once dead, my cat would feast upon the bounteous flesh that is my worldly tabernacle. So when (and yes, I said when) I die via cat, don't cry for me. I'm happy about it. Really. As far as ways to die go, having my cat kill me seems right.

My long-time cat is named Rocella; named after Barbie in the classic film *Barbie: Island Princess*, thanks to my daughter. Rocella is a very sweet cat; one I believe would never knowingly kill me. I hope. Perhaps she is so sweet because she was a feline octomom, delivering eight babies in one pregnancy. Having eight sets of teething biting at your nipples and eight bodies climbing over you would develop a keen sense of patience in anyone. Or a bout of infanticide. It is entirely possible she is just an angel by nature. Whatever the reason, Rocella is much nicer than her new little sister, Sharkeisha.

Sharkeisha was named by my fiancée, in honour of a viral video in which a bully named Sharkeisha attacks a girl without warning, prompting the surrounding people to shout, "Sharkeisha, no!" The name stuck, perhaps because of all the times we found ourselves shouting 'no!' or asking one another, a wary eye out, if they had seen the kitty, and "is it safe to cross the room?"

Sharkeisha has a nasty habit of hiding around corners and within crevices, waiting for unsuspecting victims to walk past. Once they do, she launches herself out like a leopard toward its prey, arms extended and claws out. As I write this, my entire body is an abstract art piece of red cuts on white canvas. Terrified screams are often heard by neighbours, followed by, "Ouch! You fucker!" And still, we can't help but love Sharkeisha.

When we first adopted her, she had a serious case of diarrhoea, which, while unpleasant for her, was worse for me. Not only was it irritating to constantly wash the sheets, but the very sound of diarrhoea at 2:30 in the morning is something to fear. I would wake up, wondering why someone was squirting ketchup out of a bottle (right by my head, no less) in the middle of the night. Then the stench would hit.

Sharkeisha was very small when she came to live with us and developed a (then) adorable habit of suckling on my earlobe, thinking it was a nipple. When she fit in my hand and had little baby teeth, it was charming. When she became the size of a cantaloupe and had the teeth of a sabre-toothed tiger, it was remarkably less so. I developed scabs on the lobes of my ears and walked around looking like I had a peculiar case of scabies. No matter what precautions I took, I still couldn't get her to stop.

If I put a blanket over my head, she will burrow under it, developing liquid like properties enabling her to fit through the spaces. If I try to cover everything except a small portion of nose and mouth for breathing, she will sit right by the created airhole, smothering me in cat butt until I am forced to wiggle around to breathe. The moment I move even an inch, she will take the opportunity to dive in, finding my ear with Navy Seal like marksman skill. Eventually, tired of swatting her away, I give in, letting her suckle until she falls asleep with a sigh, purring loudly the entire time.

Sharkeisha lives up to her name, bullying poor Rocella. When she isn't taking flying leaps or dives onto Rocella's back, she is hogging the food bowl or biting at Rocella's ears. For the most part, Rocella takes it like a champ; a dignified, old British lady rather than Sharkeisha's teenage gang member. Occasionally fur will fly, and poor Rocella will beg to be let out of the house, willing and ready to brave the coyotes and owls; anything to escape the little shit Sharkeisha.

Sharkeisha will have her way, no matter the situation. If there is food to be had, she will find a way to get it. Whether that means climbing up the pants of the nearest 'food pole' i.e. leg, and snatching it right out of a mouth, or sneaking a claw onto the plate and performing the ole snatch and dash. I once chased Sharkeisha across the house after she stole a chicken strip right off my plate. Yes, I still ate it. And I made her watch.

If she isn't practicing cat burglary (see what I did there?), to end her food lust, she is meowing like she was just run over by a car. Her deathlike yowls are enough to get anyone to give in. Anything to stop the noise. Go ahead and judge me all you want for 'rewarding' bad behaviour. You haven't heard her call. Your eardrums are still intact.

She also happens to have an obsession with water. This means she has subsequently fallen into the toilet several times, spraying toilet water everywhere in her frantic attempts to get out. Slipping into the tub is another matter entirely, due to the deep sides and deeper water. Unfortunately for me, I am usually relaxing in the tub when she decides to take her dip into uncharted territory. This results in me trying to get a grip on a wet cat, while she claws her way up my back in a painful (to me) escape. I'm left with a bloody back and a ruined evening of relaxation. She is left smelling like Berry Island Breeze bubble bath. Not a fair trade.

Shortly after my fiancé neglected to fix a leak (this is a story for another time), I hung up several Damp Rid packs to absorb the excess water that had seeped into the walls and floors. Sharkeisha decided these were toys to bat, bite, and poke holes in. One minute I'm resting peacefully in bed, the next I'm trying to help my kitten, who seems to be freaking out while foaming at the mouth. How does one help a terrified and foaming kitten without being clawed half to death? Hell if I know, though she seemed to have survived the ordeal with energy to spare, which she uses to bat, bite, and poke holes in other forbidden items.

She also uses that excess energy to vomit on the carpet, her favorite time to do so being night. I personally believe she prefers to barf at night knowing that I will head to the bathroom at 4 a.m., step on it, think I've just squashed a mouse, freak out, and lose my balance. I think her hope is to kill me. She wants me dead, a feast for her at the ready.

Sharkeisha wants me dead. I know it. I see it in her slow blinking gaze, her proudly sharpened claws, and her ear nibble, which grows more and more venomous every day.

The Men's Room

The first time I ever entered a men's restroom, I did it on purpose. I imagine I am not the only young lady who has been curious about what a men's restroom looks like, but there are probably very few girls out there who say to themselves, "I wonder what a man's bathroom looks like. I'm going to go investigate. At the church."

Whether it was a dare, or just rampant stupidity, I can't recall. But I do remember looking around before entering, making sure no one saw me, an obvious female, sneaking into forbidden territory.

Once inside, seeing no feet under the one toilet stall, I breathed a sigh of relief. To my surprise, they only had one toilet stall. Along the side of the wall were some strange rectangular sink looking things, which I discovered were what I had once heard referred to as 'urinals'. I wondered how men sat on them, and if they were embarrassed that other people could see them. As I was pondering the complexities of the male urinal, I heard voices in the hall.

Quickly, I hopped into the stall and locked the door just as the bathroom door opened behind me. I sat on the toilet and looked at my shoes, grateful that they were somewhat gender neutral and wouldn't give me away. I sat in silence, awkwardly listening to the sound of a zipper coming undone.

Fighting the curiosity to peep out the crack of the door and see how he was sitting on the urinal, I was startled when I heard him say, "How's it going in there?"

Inwardly, my mind buzzed a mile a millisecond. Was he talking to me? Obviously. I was the only one in here with him, right? Would he recognize me as a girl if I answered? Should I mumble? No, I was smart, and one thing I knew for sure is that every ten-year-old sounds like a girl. I responded in my normal voice.

"Um, good."

"Cool. Cool." The sound of urine hitting the urinal made me blush uncontrollably. "So, you going number one or number two?"

Once again, my mind whorled with possibilities. What did he mean by this 'number one' or 'number two'? I used the skill of deduction and determined he meant poop or pee. I couldn't say I was peeing (was that number one?) because he would wonder why I was doing it in the toilet reserved for poop. And why did he want to know? Was he a creep? The kind we are warned about in school?

"Uh, number two..." I provided, hoping this conversation would end before he suggested I show him my progress or some other equally untoward option.

"Cool. That's really cool, man."

I made a face to myself. Is that what men talked about in the bathroom? What exactly was cool about a number two? Also, was he suggesting it smelled bad in here? Did I stink? I lifted an arm and smelled the pit. I seemed fresh enough.

I held my breath and waited for him to finish. At long last, I heard his zipper zip up and the tell-tale sound of feet shuffling.

"Well, little dude, good luck with your number two."

"Uh, thanks." I blushed furiously. And with that, I heard the door open and close, no hand washing or flushing necessary apparently. *It must be nice to be a guy*, I thought. *No social norms to bog down life as a male.*

I counted to ten, figuring he needed a few minutes to get down the hallway and out of sight before I could emerge. At ten, I burst out of the stall, flying past the startled face of a man who must have entered the restroom when the other exited. There he stood, dong in hand, and mouth wide open.

Blond ponytail flying, I stumbled to the door, reminding myself that now was not the time to see what a penis looked like. That was bad. I ran outside, knowing I needed to hide, and do so quickly. If he identified me to my parents, I was doomed. I did the smartest thing I could think to do, running straight into the women's bathroom. I'd be safe there. Surely no man had ever crossed that border.

Thankfully, I was safe, as the poor man was either too embarrassed or too shocked to do any investigating into who the little pervert girl in the men's restroom was. I hid in that bathroom until my mom came looking for me, some 45 minutes later, wondering how my Sunday school class was.

"Oh, it was very educational," I said, smiling to myself at my little joke.

"So you learned something?" She asked, most likely smelling my bullshit a mile away.

"Yes," I said. *You have no idea*, I thought.

After that harrowing experience, I gained some street cred amongst fellow girls. I would, when previously cleared by a male scout, take the gals into the men's bathroom on a tour.

"Those are called urinals," I would say smugly. "They stand up to pee in them, not sit down." The girls would oooh and ahhh, and I would begin to tell them of the time I saw a man pee. To ten-year-old girls, I was a god. All knowing and mysteriously fascinating.

I would find myself in men's bathrooms often throughout the years. Usually on accident (always embarrassing) and occasionally on purpose (I really had to go). If I was ever caught using the men's room by another man, I would state that I was merely identifying as a man, desiring a shorter restroom line. Luckily that usually got a few laughs. Men don't seem to be as creeped out by a female using their toilet as women are when men do a similar thing. Sorry men, ya'll seem to have a poor track record.

On my trips into the land of men's restrooms, I have discovered that women are much messier than men. They throw paper towels, drop hair like they've developed a case of severe and sudden alopecia, and leave make up smears and blood splatters everywhere. Women's restrooms could easily be confused as active crime scenes.

Women also have an unpleasant habit of unashamedly talking on the phone while on the toilet. I once heard a woman talking for several minutes about how moist a cake she ate was, whilst dropping a few little 'moist cakes' of her own into the toilet below.

Because women talking on the phone in the bathroom is so common, I challenge myself to be as loud and obnoxious as possible, hoping to embarrass them into getting off the phone. I will make loud farting noises or flush the toilet multiple times, hoping the person on the other line will exclaim in disgust, "You are talking to me in the bathroom? Gross! What is wrong with you?" Sadly, I've never heard anyone seem to care. I hate this generation of toilet talkers.

For me, I don't need the phone, finding enough entertainment in reading the bathroom stall graffiti. When teaching at schools, I'll see the typical 'I love Chris', or 'Kelsey is a bitch' scratched onto the toilet paper holders and stall doors. Depending on the school, I may even see a 'Fuck Mr Roberts' written with 'I did last night' scrawled underneath. Those are my favorite—the ones with a continuation of comments; the Reddit of wall art.

One day in middle school, after having been hit in the face by a fellow student, I wrote graffiti of my own, while crying about the injustices of middle school life. I imagined myself building a secret spot the stall, never attending an actual class, but playing games of tic tac toe, and reading books inside my toilet nook instead of studying science and social studies.

Had I known how disgusting middle school bathrooms were, I would have rethought that plan. As it was, I didn't have long to ponder it—the vice principal came in shortly after and dragged me out of my safe haven—giving me detention instead of an apology for the slug in the face I had gotten fifteen minutes before. Like I said, injustice.

As far as I'm concerned, bathrooms can be a place of education. Be it graffiti or seeing a dick for the first time, I've learned a thing or two in there. All while going number two. Or number one. Either way, It's cool man, cool.

Psychopath

It is no exaggeration to say that I was a terrible kid. When my siblings offer stories of things that I have done, I pretend I don't know what they are talking about, though in truth, I am sure that I did it. Not long ago a cousin of mine told me her favorite memory of me was when I swore and threw a hamburger to the ground and stepped on it. For the life of me, I don't recall this. Does it sound plausible? Like something an eight-year-old me would have done? Absolutely.

I honestly don't know how my parents handled me. If I had a child like me, I would have sent them to a Buddhist Monastery before the age of four. Or had them committed. Whichever. Truthfully, I don't even understand myself. When I look back at some of the truly psychotic things that I have done, I question myself.

I know I've mentioned it before, but I'm a pretty sensitive person. Usually this plays to my favor, because it means I am more empathetic to others. Unfortunately, I can also be quite dramatic when my hormones are surging in just the right (wrong) way. As a young girl, I would do almost anything for attention. Usually this meant I had to do something so over the top that it would be noticed. Add my desire for attention with my penitent for insanity, and you get me. (Thankfully drugs have tamed the crazy a bit).

When I was eleven, I seemed to hit a particularly aggressive bullying streak. This was directed only at my siblings, because even back then I knew I had power over no one but people younger than me, who would be forced to forgive me. Via proximity or my parents.

I truly feel terrible for some of the things I did, and for others, I have no remorse. I suppose I could quite easily be a psychopath, since I seem to have little guilt for the many times I wrestled my youngest brother down and tried to get him to eat scabs. Don't worry, he got his revenge by peeing on my leg in front of my friend in the 7th grade. So I guess we are even.

I do, however, feel bad for what I did to a bear my mom gave me at Christmas. I don't remember what happened or why I was so angry, but I decided I would bury a butcher knife in the bear's back and squirt ketchup all over its back: a grisly crime scene. I left it in my bed for my mom to find. Heaven only knows what she thought when she pulled back the sheets to see that. Have I mentioned I love my mom? I cannot believe she hasn't disowned me a million times over.

Ask my sister, and she will tell you about the time I told her I was going to teach her a magic trick. The trick required me tying her to a chair with multiple jump ropes. Then, magically, I disappeared, leaving her tied to the chair until someone (not me) came to rescue her. She also likes to bring up the time my siblings and I chased her around with a knife, going so far as to corner her in a neighbour's garage. How the police didn't become involved, I'll never know. Now that I think about it, there are a lot of stories involving me and knives. I wonder what that means.

I would also go out of my way to terrify my siblings, dressing up in Halloween costumes and pretending I had broken into the house. I also enjoyed pretending I was dead, attempting to control my breathing so they would think I had entered into the land beyond. Surprisingly, I never once heard them exclaim joy at my passing. They must be better people than I am.

In school I was no better, and I'm positive several teachers probably wished for my demise. I was very well behaved until fourth grade. I decided I hated my teacher, Mr Wilson.

I have no idea why I disliked him, but he was my first ever male teacher, and for some reason I hated his attitude almost as much as he hated mine. We had a give and take, mostly to the tune of me giving him as much if not more than he could take. I'd push and push and push until he snapped.

The day he snapped I will never forget. I was in a mood, wanting to be a little asshole, and to make my friends laugh. During story time, I took a marker and wrote: 'do not write on this chair' on the back of my chair. My friends gave me shocked little giggles, then quickly looked away when Mr Wilson's eyes followed the sound.

"Laura! Did you write on that chair?" I was surprised at how nervous his bellow made me. Normally, the most I got was an irritated reprimand, barely louder than normal. This time, his voice resounded like an angry god's, and I felt shivers up my spine.

Refusing to let my class see my terror, I raised my hands in a shrug.

"I was worried someone would write on the chair, so I put a warning on there."

He exploded, "Out of all the cockeyed idiotic things I've seen students do, this is a new level of stupid! Do you actually have a brain? I mean, do you? Because I have seen absolutely no evidence of one the entire year you've been in my class! You will stay in at recess and clean every single desk and chair in the classroom. When you are done, you will clean the chalkboard. And when you finish that, you'll come with me to call your parents! Do you understand me?"

The silence in that room was palpable. You could almost taste it, the bitterness of pennies and the tang of blood. But that may have been actual blood. When he yelled, it startled me so bad, I bit open the inside of my cheek.

I stared at him, and he at me. It was do or die time, and I had to save face. Desperately, I tried to think of a clever comeback. Alas, I couldn't think of one. He was right. There was no evidence of a brain inside my head. I decided to put an end to our feud.

"Perfectly," I stated, then stared in horror as bloody spittle flew from my mouth and landed on his chin. I froze. He froze. The class froze.

"Out!" he raged, pointing for the class to go to recess while simultaneously wiping saliva out of his facial hair. The class moved faster than I had ever seen, some giving me looks of pity, knowing I would be dead before recess was over. I nodded at them, accepting their condolences.

When they were gone, Mr Wilson left for a moment. I tried to get right with God, because I knew that if he didn't kill me, my dad surely would. I didn't dare to move until I felt a rag hit me in the back of the head. I turned and watched as

Mr Wilson set down a bucket. Water sloshed over the top, and he stepped back, as if he didn't trust himself to not kill me if he got too close.

"Get started. Do not talk to me. Don't even look at me. I want everything in here to shine. You will stay after school and we will talk to your parents."

With that, he sat at his desk and dared me to protest. I did not. I feared for my safety. Worse still, I knew I deserved to. I was an ass, and I was getting what I deserved. I want to say that this is when I turned my life around, but I didn't. I have many more stories of a similar nature.

While I was a little psychopath in the making, it wasn't all knives, chair defacement, and scab eating. I also had a master plan to run away. Whenever I decided life was too hard to handle (every week or so), I would continue my plan for escape.

I planned to live in the sewers. Yes, you read that right. The sewers. Near our church was a creek with a huge concrete tunnel that lead into more concrete tunnels. They always had a small amount of water in them, but I figured I could get by with piles of leaves and tree branches. I would lay them down, and the moisture would stay off, and I'd have a soft bed.

Never mind that this was in Northern Iowa, where it easily fell below zero several times each winter. I determined that when I wasn't living the life of a teenage mutant ninja turtle, I'd be hiding out in the nearby church building. Having been forced to attend church every week without fail, I knew the ins and outs of that building. I knew that I could avoid detection by hiding in curtains, under pews, and under the stage where they stored all of the metal chairs. I had options.

I also relied on the church building for my food plans. I had planned to forage in dumpsters near the local McDonald's for leftover food and supplies for my fort. I determined that a plastic bag could be used for everything from a blanket to a water bucket. I planned to hoard garbage better than the dump. Eventually I'd collect so much I could make a fort, walls out of beer bottles and popsicle sticks, with a roof of potato chip bags and old dental floss.

Part of me has always wanted to live the simple life of a hobo. But a bigger part of me enjoys long hot baths and toilet paper. I never did run away and live with rats and mutated sewer animals, but I always had the plan with me to keep me company and to comfort me when things got tough. I knew that I had a second life just waiting for me. I still do this when I'm overly stressed. I imagine my life as a runaway, (though I think at this age I'm just considered homeless) with no responsibilities but staying alive. In a way, it is therapeutic, and short of stabbing people or forcing them to eat my old skin, I'd say I'm doing good.

Thankfully, I have lived my life relatively crime free, and have avoided any psychopathic actions. It may be true that I am not the best at keeping the speed limit, but I haven't kidnapped anyone and kept them in a little well while planning to make a suit out their skin. So I'm doing good. As far as I'm concerned, I'm a goddamn model citizen.

Letter to My Ex-Husband's New Wife

I just want you to know that I tried, I really did. I went out of my way to make your life easier, to make you feel like part of our broken family. I found you friends, who speak your language and are from your same country, I made you treats, offered to help teach you English, and let you know that I was, in no uncertain terms, friendly. A good person. Someone who wanted to work together for the good of the kids.

But you went ahead and screwed it all up.

I won't go into your actions, because when it comes down to it, they don't really matter. What matters is this:

You will never be free of me. My ghost will haunt you throughout your entire life with your new husband.

I will never actively bother you, because I'm tired. Actual haunting takes time and effort, both of which I don't want to spend on you. Maybe when you become an adult, you'll understand what that means.

I want you to know that everything in your current life has been touched by me. My ass has sat in and probably farted on every chair in your home; the home that was mine before it was yours. When you lay in your bed, know I was there before. Probably just as unhappy as you. That goes with the territory of marrying who you did. And who I did. Before you.

When you look at the walls, know that I painted them. As you pull out kitchen cabinets, remember that I installed the knobs. Every time you step on the floor, realize that I pulled up the carpet in that home so that the hardwood could be installed. I hung the pictures and décor you look at every day. I bought the towels you use when you get out of the shower I showered in.

I planted the flowers and the trees in your yard. I built the brick garden wall, and I painted the front door. I installed the door and light fixtures. I mowed the lawn.

Your (my) dog loved me first, and so did your husband. (gag). My kids, while I hope they can maintain a decent relationship with you, will never love you the way they love me. Those are the cards you are dealt when you marry into a separated family.

I'm sure you are laughing; knowing that you are in a McMansion in a rich area while I am in a mobile home in a bad part of town. You've got the neighbourhood pool, and I have neighbourhood shootings.

Here's the thing: I've been where you are. I've lived in the McMansion, I've swam in the neighbourhood pool, and I, (as much as I hate to admit it) married your husband. And guess what? I'd give it all up again and again to have the happiness I have now.

I am with someone who doesn't make me feel alone. He treats me fairly and communicates properly. He helps me with household chores, and he doesn't treat me like shit. I'm so lucky that I have what I do. And that I got rid of what you now have.

Part of me wants to feel sorry for you. Soon your honeymoon phase will be over and you will realize you married an idiot. You will be stuck in a new country with few connections and a thin grasp of the language. You will be saddled with two children that are not your own, and work that you never wanted to do.

You will be mowing the lawn while your husband takes naps. You'll be cooking and cleaning while he watches sports for hours on end. You'll feel resentment build up and feel hopelessly trapped.

Perhaps, after you have wasted ten years of your life, you will decide to divorce. You will fight for custody and spend thousands of dollars you don't have on a lawyer who doesn't do jack shit to help. You'll fire your lawyer and agree to your soon to be ex-husband's greedy terms. You'll find a shitty job that pays terribly just to pay him child support. You fought for the kids, but he had more money to fight with. So you'll lose. You'll feel like you lost everything.

Then, after all that, you just may be living in a tiny apartment somewhere. Maybe even a mobile home. And you'll remember my words. Because after all that time, all those years, I'm still haunting you.

BOO BITCH.

CPSIA information can be obtained
at www.ICGtesting.com
Printed in the USA
LVHW080048271021
701610LV00010B/221